PRAISE FOR BEL MOONEY

'An enchanting book – heart-breaking, but also heart-making.'
JOANNA LUMLEY

'A moving and honest story of the end of a marriage … rich, rare and engrossing.'
ANTONIA FRASER

'Bel Mooney is a courageous woman with an unbelievably generous heart.'
RICHARD HOLLOWAY, AUTHOR AND FORMER BISHOP OF EDINBURGH

'I could not put this book down.'
VANESSA FELTZ

'This dignified, generous, loving portrayal of the break-up of a
long marriage is one many people will empathise with…'
TRISHA ASHLEY, NOVELIST

'In this time of confessional writing I have never read such an honest, evocative
account …The way Bel Mooney describes the ageing process and coming to
terms with what has happened in order to move on feels so relevant.'
JOANNE GOOD, ACTRESS AND BBC RADIO PRESENTER

'A profound disquisition … Buried in this novel is the stuff of greatness.'
STEPHEN GLOVER, *DAILY TELEGRAPH*

'An impressive return to fiction. The ease with which Mooney handles both big
ideas and smaller intimacies makes you hope she won't leave it so long next time.'
MELISSA KATSOULIS, *THE TIMES*

'Deep questions, and Mooney is not afraid to tackle them head-on. She writes
sensitively and tenderly … a remarkably good novelist.'
GOOD HOUSEKEEPING

Bel Mooney's
LIFELINES

ALSO BY BEL MOONEY

NOVELS:

The Windsurf Boy
The Anderson Question
The Fourth of July
Lost Footsteps
Intimate Letters
The Invasion of Sand

NON-FICTION:

The Year of the Child
Bel Mooney's Somerset
Differences of Opinion (journalism)
Perspectives for Living (Radio 4 programmes)
Devout Sceptics (Radio 4 programmes)
A Small Dog Saved My Life (memoir)

FOR CHILDREN:

The Stove Haunting
A Flower of Jet
Joining the Rainbow
The Voices of Silence
Mr Tubs Is Lost
Who Loves Mr Tubs?
Promise You Won't Be Cross
The Mouse With Many Rooms
Luke and the Green Man
The 'Kitty' series
The 'Bonnie' series

Bel Mooney's
LIFELINES
Words to Help You Through

The Robson Press

First published in Great Britain in 2015 by
The Robson Press (an imprint of Biteback Publishing Ltd)
Westminster Tower
3 Albert Embankment
London SE1 7SP
Copyright © Bel Mooney 2015

ISBN 978-1-84954-932-5

10 9 8 7 6 5 4 3 2 1

A CIP catalogue record for this book is available from the British Library.

Set in Goudy Oldstyle

Printed and bound in Great Britain by
CPI Group (UK) Ltd, Croydon CR0 4YY

For Sandra Parsons, without whom this would not have happened

Loveless hearts shall love tomorrow, hearts that
have loved shall love anew,
Spring is young now, spring is singing, in the spring
the world first grew.

Anonymous – Latin (c. fourth century)

…if you picture other people like you, you will no longer be
alone. And when you share, you see that your own sorrow is not
so big or special. You are only another person feeling sad, and
soon it will pass and you will be another person feeling happy.

From *The Love Song of Miss Queenie Hennessy* by Rachel Joyce

After the final No there comes a Yes,
And on that Yes the future of the world depends.

Wallace Stevens

CONTENTS

INTRODUCTION

BEGINNINGS

IT WAS NEVER a part of my life plan to write a newspaper advice column. That fact just serves to prove what I often say to readers – if you aren't willing to open yourself up to the unexpected, you could miss out being (in Wordsworth's phrase) 'surprised by joy'. That's how it was with me, in 2005, when my first advice column appeared in *The Times*. Despite initial doubts, I soon realised this was going to be a new vocation. I had been afraid that I couldn't do it, that it would be depressing, that I would become imprisoned by the problems of others. It also worried me that I might be accused of being unqualified – even though it's rather hard to define exactly what are the best qualifications for an 'agony aunt' (a title I dislike, as it patronises all concerned). What does it take to give advice to perfect strangers?

Then I thought, OK – I've been cheated and mistreated (as the Everly Brothers sang) and bullied and insecure and lonely and bereaved. I've behaved shamefully in the past but I've also done things along the way that make me proud. A sinner and a saint – yeah, that's about right.

Growing up, I became aware of painful family problems. Raised in a Liverpool council flat, I am lucky enough (as a baby boomer) to epitomise social mobility. I married young and had three children, one of whom was stillborn. I cared for my sick daughter for many years and spent more time in hospitals than I would wish on anyone. My long career has contained some bitter disappointments but I learned to put them in perspective. In middle age, I endured the sudden collapse of my very long marriage and had to rebuild my life. A second marriage has brought me more contentment than I could have imagined. Now, in my seventieth year, I face ageing and think about death perhaps more than I should. In my life I've read a whole library of books, taken deep pleasure in art and music and interviewed countless people – all of this confirming what I probably realised subliminally as a child: that human existence is complex, interesting, disappointing, frightening, puzzling, mundane – and more full of quiet desperation than blazing joy.

After some thought, therefore, I realised I was as qualified as anybody to engage with the problems of others. A line in Virgil's *Aeneid* sums up the thought: 'Familiar with grief, I learn to help the unhappy.'

So, I began the new job. The *Times* column (called 'Life and Other Issues') quickly established itself and at first the letters and emails often made me weep or sometimes exclaim aloud in fury. How could people be so petty, so cruel, so lacking in self-awareness? And how can a human being (the one who wrote that pitiful letter I held in my hand) sustain such soul-sapping misery? For years I had contributed features and comment to the paper (and indeed to most national papers and many magazines), yet a freelance journalist is rarely party to his or her readers' private realities. You write your article, possibly get feedback (before the days of online comment, this wasn't common) then move on to the next assignment. But an advice columnist is quickly 'in there' with readers. I found that, with the safety that comes from talking to a stranger, people would often open up to me more than perhaps to a friend or family member, disclosing extremely intimate information about their lives.

It wasn't long before I saw how the problems divided into categories. Listed in order of volume, they stack up like this:

On marriage – from women.

On relationships – from women.

On family problems – from men and women.

On marriage and relationships – from men.

On bereavement – from men and women.

On … just … *angst*. Loneliness, a sense of pointlessness and the question: 'Why on earth are we living?'

Letters also arrived about problems with work and friendships, but not nearly so many. Painstakingly, I chose different subjects each week to keep the page fresh, although it won't surprise you to hear that I could have easily written about bad and sad marriages and nothing else. At first, I felt overwhelmed by the misery – and horribly responsible. How do you cope upon receiving a pitiful, handwritten letter in which the writer says they're so miserable they want to 'end it all' – worse, when there is no address to write back to? It was extremely distressing. One thing that surprised me, however, was an odd, 'witchy' sixth sense that led me to surmise this or that about the writer of a letter and incorporate those second guesses in a printed reply – and then hear back from them: 'How did you *know?*' Perhaps a literary training is just as useful as a counselling course – for reading between the lines and weighing the import of specific words chosen.

Some readers' responses were very moving. For example, a man wrote to tell me that one year earlier he had read a letter in my column from a guy who was about to leave his wife for his mistress. Children were involved and so (mindful of the damage that can be done) I counselled extreme caution. But, just imagine – somewhere in Britain this *other* man was reading my words – addressing his own identical dilemma. That man studied my advice, pondered, and decided to stay with his wife. Then he waited a whole year before writing to tell me that it had worked – the advice and the marriage both. The intervening time had been tough but he and his wife had talked and sought help and talked some more ... and he now knew they would stay together. So at last, he wrote, it was time to say thank you. Is it that surprising my husband found me snuffling quietly in front of my computer?

The realisation that this new job could be so useful made me humble. And when an unhappy man or woman closes a very, very long screed with, 'Just writing this down and knowing you will read it has helped me', I feel quietly glad to provide the outlet. When people are used to communicating by text or brief emails, sitting down to write a long letter (on paper or keyboard) can be cathartic. But editing such missives is my nightmare – and it makes replying harder, in a way, because I possess more knowledge than can appear on the page. Sometimes readers will write to question the judgement that I've made based on this knowledge – but, hey, nobody ever said this job was easy.

Given the time and effort I put into the column, therefore, it should come as no surprise how frustrated and irritated I feel when an unthinking person (perhaps at a party or a book signing) asks the cliché question: 'Are the letters real?' Do they not realise that it's crass to suggest that my editor and I are con-merchants pretending to offer a helpful service? I fight the impulse to riposte, 'I've written fiction and know the difference!' – remaining polite. But I imagine inviting such cynics to visit my office at home and chucking a pile of letters or emails (always printed out for me to study) over his or her head, while yelling 'Real? You want *real*? Feel the weight of that lot!'

HONESTY

When, after two years, I moved from *The Times* to the *Daily Mail*, there were more letters from a far larger and broader readership, yet the issues that kept men and women awake at night were the same. I became even more convinced that readers don't want advice on emotional problems dealt out (as it were) from the anonymous safety of the confessional. When I looked at other problem pages (some written by well-qualified teams and doing an excellent job, but most by individuals who are equally dedicated) I noticed how they kept a distance. To be truthful, it's not that hard to dish out advice based on the practical wisdom in a guide to relationships or one of the useful self-help books that abound. Nowadays, you can research website contacts and pass them on. It's all good, all valuable – and I know advice columns can be very, very helpful – but only if written in a spirit that respects those who send the letters. In those early days, however, I met an established advice columnist at a party who airily waved away my earnest little questions with a casual, 'Oh, just send them all off to counselling.' Not good enough, I thought.

I wanted to be more honest, more personal. Surely an advice column might be a spectator sport – unless readers know you're in the team too? During a long career, I've been a columnist for many newspapers and magazines, poured out my soul into six novels for adults, and conducted moving interviews for radio and television about bereavement and God (to name but two subjects). In none of it could I keep my distance. Glad to wear the heart-shaped team colours on my sleeve, I reached middle age immune to po-faced reservations about 'personal journalism' because of a certain pride that said heart was still exposed – bashed about, but beating as strongly as ever. How can you disguise the wobble in your voice when you feel moved during a radio interview? What is wrong with reaching out to people, just as you want them to reach right back to you? I discovered how powerfully my readers responded to stories from my own life and realised that to do the job well I had to give as much of my 'all' as it is possible to give.

Because the collapse (after thirty-five years) of my marriage to a well-known writer and broadcaster had been played out in public, readers felt they *knew* me. My 2010 memoir *A Small Dog Saved My Life* dealt frankly with the end of that marriage, as well as dogs as a force for healing – and prompted even more readers to write and say, 'I know you've been through this too, so…' Because I've been the subject of many profiles in newspapers and magazines over the years, they would comment, 'I know you weren't born with a silver spoon in your mouth, so…' And the long history of 'personal journalism' helped too. For example, I once wrote a significant article about the agony of stillbirth (it appeared in *The Guardian* on 8 January 1976 and had far-reaching effects) and now, in this new incarnation as advice columnist, women found it easy to pour out their hearts to me when they lost their babies. And so on.

I discovered that the more I gave the more I received. Listen, people, I'd say (in different ways) – we're all in this together, and believe me, a good education, house and job is no protection against pain. Believe me, I know.

LESSONS

My column appears in the hefty Saturday edition of the *Daily Mail*, with a potential readership of over six million people. I read, choose and edit all the letters myself – from readers who have ranged in age from a nine-year-old to the late nineties. They send problems, of course – but also letters of thanks, pretty cards carrying blessings, pictures of a beloved and much-missed spouse, sometimes with copies of touching wedding snaps in wartime. They send favourite poems, book recommendations and comments on what they have read, often sharing their own stories. They write about loneliness, longing and loss. From time to time (but very rarely) I receive a dose of abuse too – but this goes with the territory. A man whose wife has treated him badly will transfer his hatred of her on to me and berate me for 'hating men' (as if!). A woman will flex her bitchiest muscles to sneer – just because she has a different view from one I expressed on the page. We can't all agree. Does it annoy me when people are rude? Yes. There's no excuse for it, but the internet has coarsened discourse forever. In general, I realise how unhappy they are and make allowances. You have to cut some slack to wounded creatures who snarl.

'What is the worst problem?' people ask, or 'Is there something you've learned from all the letters?' Thinking of the sheaves of handwriting and stacks of computer printouts in boxes and cupboards within my untidy study, and unwilling to generalise, I say 'no'. Once, a man clocked up 5,000 words pouring out the agony of his marriage in greater detail than even I had ever seen. Unusually, I emailed to ask if he'd be prepared to edit himself, because I thought the exercise might be helpful. Pleased by such attention, he came back with the stipulated 500 words, which I then printed. Yet I was haunted by the complexity of that first rambling letter – which, in my mind's eye, appeared as a long corridor of locked doors, behind any one of which might have been the happy marriage he dreamed of, when first in love. His cries of anger and pain echoed in that corridor and nothing could help his wounded spirit – doomed to wander forever searching the lost room that would offer him rest and peace.

Sometimes I think this is the key to human life – that there is no key.

What do I find most heart-breaking about the letters I read each week? The fact that people are so stuck. Marooned. Entrapped. I visualise a helpless creature in a cage, holding the bars and sometimes rattling them in despair, looking out with pleading eyes, longing for escape.

One of my favourite poets, T. S. Eliot, writes, 'We think of the key, each in his prison / Thinking of the key…' As a teenager I loved the Joan Baez song, 'There But for Fortune' which begins, 'Show me the prison, show me the jail, show me the prisoner whose life has gone stale…' and hammers home the message of empathy and compassion: 'There but for fortune go you or I.' Years later, I still believe that we might all share the same fate, if it were not for accidents of parentage and tricks of destiny.

So, no judgements from me. Oh – apart from when somebody drives me mad. There are people who don't want to be helped, but clutch their misery to their chests. The key to a (possible) new life doesn't always lie in any help from outside, but in that locked-up victim deciding to seek a way out all by him or herself. And that's when I might decide to use 'tough love'. A critical reader once wrote to inform me that one or two of my replies were 'too prescriptive' – which 'therapists and counsellors' are not supposed to be. But listen, lady (I wrote back), I am not one of those! If readers ask me what I think, I will tell them – from my heart. Just as I would a friend. What's the point of lazy sympathy? 'There, there … poor old thing … you must do what you think best'? I have been called 'bloody stupid' in my time by a friend who wanted to make me see the error of my ways – so I sometimes dish that thought out too, although not in so many words.

I try to suggest solutions, to be helpful – even inspirational. But if men and women choose to remain locked up there is little you can do. Of course, you can advise counselling (that useful catch-all) but many people turn their backs on the suggestion, because, I suspect, they don't want somebody to sit with them and slowly, carefully point out other ways of looking. (Nevertheless, I do often recommend the 'talking cure' just as that veteran advice columnist told me, because just making the first appointment is a step towards taking control.) Perhaps the fear is understandable, yet it can be rooted in ignorant prejudice too, as if there is shame in admitting you may be wrong. Sometimes they will be embarrassed – and that's when I want to cry out through the page (or computer screen), 'Look, I've been there too! I've gone to a stranger for help. Believe it – and just try listening!' In the words of the American poet Mary Oliver, 'Tell me about despair, yours, and I will tell you mine. Meanwhile the world goes on.'

From time to time I've done a short course, to learn from others. I read books on mindfulness and happiness and spiritual quests, knowing how helpful they can be. But a key…? Ah, the great question – like the ancient wish to turn base metal into gold. I continue to read the novels and poetry that have always been the mainstay of my life, to haunt art galleries too (as I have since the age of eleven), wondering if the key to understanding is to be found there – in art. The answer is: sometimes. But not in an obvious way. You can be in a pub and hear a schmaltzy old song playing in the background, notice an elderly woman swaying to its tune with tears in her eyes and realise that this is 'art' too. For the few minutes when the dated lyric takes her back to a sacred (or possibly sexy) moment in her past, it holds the key to love and to loss, just like the ache of Schubert or Bach. The key is the moment of reaching out: the answering fizz of words or sound or image and that second when the electricity crackles across the void – and we are made one. All of us. Made one. It really is possible. But you have to open yourself to that electric shock.

Always I come back to the giving and the taking, the listening and the revealing.

OPENING OUT

The column had been running for just four months when the editor came up with an idea for 'added value'. Each week I would write a column at the side of the double page called 'And Finally'. This would give me 350 extra words (no more, no less) in which to share something important to me, or to pick up reader comments – or whatever. 'Anything you like,' he said. The idea was that this would help my page add up to *more* than a normal advice column. As well as giving sensible counsel, which often incorporated personal experience, I could write opinion and observation as well – outside the usual remit of the so-called 'agony aunt'.

So, I added anecdotes about things I had seen and done, as well as the kind of news about charities and other worthwhile organisations/initiatives for which there is usually no room in a busy, crammed newspaper like the *Daily Mail*. Most important, perhaps, I could air reader responses to printed letters and my response to them in turn – allowing the 'conversation' to open out. Genuine communication. I'd celebrate family occasions or confess to feeling tired or unhappy. At such times kind readers would write words of comfort to the woman who is supposed to be comforting *them* – thus proving there's communal consolation in all feeling 'in it' together. Sometimes a reader would stop me in the street or a shop and ask, 'How did your house move go?' because she had read my news in 'And Finally'. I never mind this; on the contrary, I love the proof that readers genuinely feel they know me through the page. It's even led to an elegant stranger pouring out her heart to me at a store opening about how her husband had walked out of their marriage, leaving her alone in her late fifties. 'I know you know,' she said. What greater compliment is there?

After a couple of years of writing 'And Finally', I suggested extra added value could come from a carefully chosen quotation – a 'thought for the week' – for the top of the column. I will seize any chance to offer inspiring words, no matter who has written them – and readers often told me they liked the quotations from great writers I included within answers. Literature has been my life since I first learned to read, so now I could pull out a line from (say) the new prize-winning novel and add it to the page, hoping readers might follow up and read the book. So now the four elements were in place: long letter, shorter letter, personal side column about anything at all and a top quotation, in poetry or prose, or occasionally a song lyric. And I should mention the picture. Each week illustrator Neil Webb interprets the main letter with imagination and a stylish sense of colour. This is the mix: something for everyone, with more general things to balance out the unhappiness of the letters.

CHANGING

Writing the column has changed me. I no longer weep at my desk – not through a hardening of the heart but simply because you have to get used to things and *bear* them, or you couldn't carry on. A nurse in a children's hospital once told me that, but at the time it was hard to understand. (My own daughter was her patient, so maybe that's why.)

But one dark January day, two letters arrived in the same batch and left me howling (not crying) on the study floor. One was from a woman whose eleven-year-old son had been killed in a road traffic accident. She had read my memoir of love and loss and identified with it and wrote to tell me of her new spiritual quest. The other came from a woman my age whose husband had walked out of the family home, which had witnessed so much happiness in earlier years, to be with his mistress. She was bereaved and bewildered – a feeling I recognised. The raw grief within both those letters left me pole-axed and I felt helpless – realising the limitations of language. No glib words of comfort could be plucked from the air and offered with a Pollyanna smile. So I wrote back to both women privately to offer a virtual embrace. What else can you do but hold out a hand – even if that hand trembles before the enormity of sorrow?

Once I had answers; now I did not. No book I had read could solve what C. S. Lewis called 'the problem of pain'. And I came to reflect (oddly enough) that running a problem page cures you of trust in the panacea of progressive politics. As a young woman I was so idealistic, and believed that with equal pay and other correct improvements of our society, the world would automatically become a better place. Politics and campaigning journalism could achieve this, I thought – and stifled my doubts, when (for example) the famous trade union leader I had interviewed was clearly a complete shit, even though on the 'right' side. Now, after ten years of writing an advice column, I have become convinced that although social improvements will help create a better society (of course, and that struggle can never cease), 'agony' is no respecter of privilege and it is fatuous to think that with the 'right' attitudes people will become better. All the liberal optimism in the world cannot salve the wounds of grief. Or teach people empathy – instructing them that you must not cross the road when you spot someone recently bereaved walking towards you. Or make people genuinely kind – beyond paying lip-service to compassion.

How can you go on believing in human, social or political perfectibility when proofs of the opposite come in every day? I'm a great admirer of the work of the late Sir Isaiah Berlin (1909–97), one of the most gifted twentieth-century political theorists and historians of ideas. This great man, who had witnessed revolutions, argued for nuance and tolerance. His writings express my feelings: a dislike of black-and-white ideas and arrogant claims to know 'the truth'. How I hate conviction! Berlin quotes with approval the eighteenth-century German philosopher Kant, who wrote: 'Out of timber so crooked as that from which man is made nothing entirely straight can be built.'

Writing my column has shown me how 'crooked' people are – not in the criminal sense, but as a tree can be bent, twisted, full of odd protuberances and flaws in the bark. No one solution fits them all.

Most of us muddle along in the centre ground, and the problem letters help me understand why. No matter how much money they have, people still mess up. How can you legislate for happiness? Yes, you can intervene and try to improve lives (of course we must – this is the Golden Rule) but if people do not want to seize whatever chances they have been given, I no longer believe that it is all the fault of society or capitalism or 'the system'. You could say I respect people too much for that. Each one of us is in charge of our own soul. Squander that sacred duty if you like, but accept some blame when you do. And – most of all – look to your children. It is there that hope must lie – and yet the advice columnist discovers how people are damaged by their parents. Horrible people use their children as emotional footballs, and then they write to me. And it all continues.

So, do I feel jaded? Yes, sometimes – when I'm drowning and yearn for my old, easy buoyancy. These days I would call myself a realist – but it doesn't seem such a bad thing. Not a cynic, at least.

Being an advice columnist has changed me in other ways too. I no longer spread myself thinly because I need to focus on *this*. What's more, I lost all desire to write fiction – even for children (and my career as a children's author had brought me enormous delight as well as success). The real stories I read every week drove out any wish to make up stories of my own. My imagination was blasted by truth. In that sense, my world has shrunk, yet how can that be when the letters have taken me into so many different worlds – some of which I would rather not enter? To do the job properly you can't be juggling a score of other things. What's more, I no longer want to travel very far – valuing my precious home and family all the more because my letters remind me every day that such blessings are not given to all.

THE SPIRIT

Since I always advise my readers to embrace change, I must do so myself. Although I have called myself an agnostic for years I find myself moving more and more towards faith – perhaps because I now fully understand the shattering, world-changing meaning of 'Love thy neighbour as thyself.' What hope is there for humanity if we do not obey that injunction? Oh, I haven't been born again – I'm still struggling along: sceptical, but devout too. However, I do believe we all need stories to help us make sense of our lives, and when the all-too-human stories I read make me sad, I must find solace somewhere. There are many good myths to live by, but I find my true home within the one that has shaped the culture I value so much. To cut to the chase – it's all there for me within the Sistine Chapel ceiling and the Sermon on the Mount: the visual and the verbal, the most sublime creativity and kindness. Since the essence of Christianity is self-sacrifice and forgiveness, I find it entirely relevant to what I do.

The pitiful, crumpled, handwritten letters I have just been reading ('I have to tell somebody this … the fifty-two years of misery … he has no compassion for me … how can I bear this life, Bel?') are a daily reminder of Auden's declaration: 'We must love one another or die.' Or the Golden Rule: 'Do unto others as you would have them do to you.' That idea is essential – and the basis of many of the ethical systems on which societies have been built. Expressions of it in various versions have existed in the classic literature of Greece and Rome, as well as in Islamic, Taoist, Sikh and other religious texts, and it nestles at the heart of Christianity. The pitilessness of the world forever calls it into question yet, tarnished though it may be, the call to greater goodness still shines in the darkness. If individuals enacted it within their own lives, there would be no more need of advice columns.

But they don't.

And won't.

No, I can no longer believe in the best, just the possibility of being – and becoming – better. Which means emotionally healed and morally 'improved'. All of us. The letters I file under 'angst' are evidence of a spiritual *need* people rarely identify. The beginning of Carol Ann Duffy's haunting poem 'Prayer' conveys the thought that the yearning, the longing, can bubble up spontaneously from deep within us: 'Some days, although we cannot pray, a prayer / utters itself.' I have a habit of suggesting little rituals readers could carry out, and frequently hear back that they *work*. This is to invoke a sort of ancient magic (you have to try something) that modernity might describe as 'autosuggestion'. But sometimes the great spiritual longing – the emptiness inside – can find expression only as a plea to God, the universe, the Tao, whatever. By all means write to an advice columnist to ask for help, but why not stand in the middle of a field and raise your head to the sky and ask for help there too? The directing of the spirit upwards and outwards (never mind its destination) can be the moment of escape from the imprisoning self. I repeat – you have to try something. It is the trying that counts, no matter how many failures occur along the way.

Now, since I have advocated honesty, I must confess something almost embarrassing: there are bright days when my own bruised spirit is healed by the realisation that I genuinely *love* my readers – these people I have never met. How odd is that? Looking at them as through a glass darkly I see my own flaws reflected back – and so what else can I do but 'preach' forgiveness? Sometimes I may cast a metaphorical stone, but only because I feel that is the most helpful thing to do, not because I feel superior to the unhappy, confused person who has written in – just more fortunate.

TRANSFORMATION

Often asked whether I intend to compile an 'anthology' of columns and/or a collection of quotations, my reply was a decisive 'No'. Then one day (after an especially loving letter of appreciation from yet another stranger calling me a friend), I thought, 'Why not?' So, to put together this book I have drawn from the 'And Finally' columns (tweaked when necessary) and also from my replies to a wide range of letters. Sometimes I have simply précised the problem; other times I've included most of the letter as well. I should emphasise that all names have been changed – I always do, even if they don't offer a pseudonym themselves.

Looking back through eight years' worth of advice columns was a strange experience and made me rather gloomy. So many problems, going round and round – the unfaithful husbands, mean daughters-in-law, lonely grandparents, restless, unhappy wives, confused children – I was reminded of something Darwin wrote: 'Selfish and contentious people will not cohere, and without coherence nothing can be effected...' Yes, indeed. How can you put your life back together if you are still stamping furiously on the fragments? How can you help your family if you are deafened by your own angry criticisms of them? Each day my postbag brings proof of self-centredness and petty conflict and malice and meanness – all evidence that the Seven Deadly Sins still thrive in this world of ours.

But, set against all that, there is also the good news of kindness and the saving power of human love. Not so long ago a woman wrote to say a heartfelt thank you to me after *five years* because, in 2010, I printed her letter on the page and advised her to stay with the erring partner whom she loved but who had wounded her grievously by using pornography and going to prostitutes. Why would you advise a woman to stay with a man like that, one might wonder? I knew most readers would disagree, but my witchy sense kicked in, and so I counselled forgiveness and hard work on the relationship. Five years later she wrote to tell me he is a changed man, and they are getting married and are 'SO happy'. This I believe in – the eternal struggle between darkness and light.

My hope is that there may be enough here to make you reflect on your own life, and possibly rethink. This miscellany of thoughts and emotions is punctuated by some of the favourite quotations I've used – which more than one reader regularly cuts out to think about for a week. You can read straight through, but I'd like to think these (mostly) short passages will be dipped into, just to see what's there. After much thought I rejected the idea of structuring the text according to subject matter, because I want the collection to be as random as fate. Sections entitled 'Marriage' or 'Family' might deter readers who could still find something interesting within a subject not obviously relevant to their own lives.

The common theme is 'Change'. Or the potential for

transformation. Just as I have changed, so I know people must change in order to push their own lives forward – after great disappointment, divorce or death. The logic is inescapable: you have to change in order to transform your life. I want readers to look back at the problem and ask, 'What have I learned?' Then look forward (how terrifying that can be?), and ask, 'How can I use this knowledge to make changes in my life and/or the lives of those around me?' This is the process we must all go through, whatever we want from life. Transformation is, after all, at the heart of fairy and folk tales and the great myths; it is a current than runs through all cultures.

You may be on your knees, desperate and lonely, but unless you accept the necessity for change, no one will be able to help you. This is the core thread that runs through all the letters I have read in ten years. The need for – and fear of – change. And even though pessimism sometimes threatens, I cling to a faith in possibility, as long as we breathe. As the great Sam Cooke sang (in 1964):

There have been times that I thought I couldn't last for long,
But now I think I'm able to carry on,
It's been a long time coming,
But I know a change is gonna come, oh yes it will.

You never step into the same river twice, and since the idea of change runs through most (if not all) of the content, like a river in full spate, there can be no divisions. So, for the most part, these extracts appear in the order they were written, but where there has been a follow-up I juxtapose it here.

If there is a particular problem besetting you, try opening the book to take a chance on what comes up. It may not be obviously relevant – but you never know what words will jump out at you, suggesting a new way of thinking about a general problem.

Let me give you an example of this glorious, accidental process. Once upon a time, utterly miserable after the irrevocable collapse of my first marriage, I walked into the John Lewis store in London's Oxford Street and noticed the early spring displays in the basement household department. They were all crowned with jolly hanging placards that said, 'RESTORE,' 'REFRESH' and 'RENEW'. I stood among the ironing boards and laundry baskets and shiny buckets in bright colours, gazing in wonder. 'NEW START' said another one – and those words told me what to do.

Writing my advice column, I sometimes feel like somebody leaning over the side of a canal holding out a stout rope to the person floundering in the water. I can't swim – and know how it feels to be in there, cold and wet and longing for the lifeline to be held out towards your desperate hands. And suddenly realising, with gratitude, that you can reach and (oh, the effort…) *reach* … and be pulled out … and that there's a friendly, protective embrace waiting to reassure you that you'll soon be warm and dry again, and that it will be all right.

It really will.

At least, I hope.

It is one of the beautiful compensations of life that no man can sincerely help another without helping himself.

Ralph Waldo Emerson (American essayist and poet, 1803–82)

I

HAPPY MIND?

The letter came from a woman who felt very low and asked me, 'Do you think it is just luck as to how optimistic or happy we are in our lives? Have you always had your happy and positive attitude?'

YOUR FINAL QUESTIONS lead me down two roads, one philosophical and one personal. But of course they are connected. I can't separate my attitude to life in general from what has happened to me – all good things, like the love of parents, as well as the bad and the sad. But then, that doesn't fully explain those amazing people who have been dealt a truly terrible hand (disability, poverty, tragedy…) yet rose above it to enjoy lives full of happiness/acceptance/forgiveness. Is that just a matter of 'luck'? Or do we make our own luck?

Let's start with your judgement on yourself that you are 'ungrateful, moaning, pathetic'. I wonder how many readers will have snapped,

'Oh, for heaven's sake, pull yourself together, woman!' But that knee-jerk reaction ignores the fact that crippling anxiety and depression are the biggest causes of misery in Britain today and (according to one professional survey) one in six of us would be diagnosed as having depression or chronic anxiety disorder.

That means that one family in three contains somebody who doesn't want to get up in the morning because he/she sees the Black Dog lurking in the corner, waiting to bite. Mental illness accounts for over one-third of the burden of illness in Britain and it's a national scandal. Many of those who go to the GP have a brief chat and then get a prescription for antidepressants (like you) when what they need is a set of appointments with a properly qualified therapist who will work with them to try to change those mental patterns. (The trouble is, who will fund this?)

You say you saw a counsellor but no 'specific problem' was identified. It sounds as if he/she wasn't much good because such permanent lowness of spirits is surely a problem. And, by the way, it's revealing that you use the phrase 'received counselling'. That's no good! Counselling is a process that you take part in. This terrible passivity is destroying you.

People often hide depression because they are ashamed. But it isn't fair that somebody who breaks a leg will receive sympathy yet somebody whose heart is fractured is given short shrift. Chirping 'Always look on the bright side of life' won't work for the person, like you, who has never seen the bright side, and finds it hard to believe it is there. I am not a psychiatrist but – yes – some people are unlucky enough to be prone to clinical depression and, even if the situation is not that acute, there are those who always look at the world through melancholy eyes, seeing the glass as half empty.

Counselling will work only if you truly want to help yourself, and I fear you don't. You don't ask me for advice as to how to change things, but sound as if you've wrapped gloom around yourself like a big, black cloak and are quite prepared to stay smothered in it until you die. Why is this? It could be genetic, but it could also be the result of things that happened to you when small. For example, were your parents and/or teachers very critical of you? This can leave people entirely negative, not believing in themselves, the world or in any worthwhile future. While you look for a therapist, cast your mind back and try to think of a reason for your unhappiness.

Just doing that will be a start, because it is a sort of 'action'. You describe your daily life as one of utter emptiness: sleeping, slobbing in front of the TV and feeling sorry for yourself. Everybody knows that two ways to keep misery at bay are: (a) to take exercise and (b) to interact with other people. It will also help if you buy a smart new notebook and do a little project – which is to write down each day a list of (say) four positive things you achieved. For example, 'Bought myself flowers; tidied underwear drawer and chucked out grey stuff; made a new dish; pulled plug on TV and played cards/ had good talk instead.'

Do it.

You'll find that most positive people have endured periods when black clouds threatened, but they refused to submit. I can remember the day over thirty years ago when I ditched prescribed tricyclic antidepressants. And in that moment I made the first step upwards out of the pit, because I was taking control – choosing pain over numbness, truth over denial, life over death.

Why make that choice? Because my mother carried me for nine months and I owed it to her. Because I love the taste of good food, the smell of jasmine, the texture of my little dog's ears, the sight of my loved ones, the sound of birdsong in my garden. So many reasons. This is more than a 'happy attitude', because my mind has little to do with it. Each day I flip the negatives ('I've put weight on around my middle') to make a positive ('But a thin face is the worst thing when you're over sixty') because I don't know any other way to be. Does that make me lucky? Sure. But I do work hard to keep that glass topped up.

Do not seek the answers, which cannot be given to you,
because you would not be able to live them. And the point is,
to live everything. Live the questions now.

Rainer Maria Rilke (Austrian poet, 1875–1926)

2

GUILT

The writer had an abortion fifteen years earlier and is still consumed with guilt, writing 'with tears running down my face'. Within my reply I 'wrapped' two others with the same problem.

THE DEBATE ABOUT abortion will never go away and the rights and wrongs do not concern me here. Your letter is about grief and guilt; you have written hoping to find some healing. Your story has terrible remorse and unresolved mourning at its core and you take full responsibility for the wrong decision. The loss of an unborn child has become the invisible cloud that blocks out the sun, or a granite weight on the soul.

I cannot answer without being personal and honest. At the end of 1980 I had a (very early) termination, for medical reasons and also because I was the mother of an eleven-month-old baby who needed constant hospital treatment. I felt no guilt; I agreed with my doctor (and husband) that it was the right thing to do. In 1975, I'd had a stillborn son – a sorrow I carry until this day – and 26 November would have been his thirty-second birthday. Two years after my abortion I was pregnant again, and miscarried. I'm telling you all this so that you know that I do not write from some safe, lofty distance, but genuinely understand the anguish of these decisions, the memory of which never goes away.

Pain is one thing: part of the human condition. Yet the kind of guilt that corrodes the edges of life, damaging all other relationships … that we must deal with. You, Katie, are hurting yourself and your husband every day. You each say you are a terrible person, when you are not. It is same for many women. Somehow or other, the little ghosts must be laid to rest, given the peace they require, in order that their mothers can go on with life. There is a whole passage about this in my last novel *The Invasion of Sand*, invoking an aboriginal belief that the dead have to be set free, in order for the living to begin life afresh. We cannot cling on to them. They need to be released.

What can I do but confide something that gave me the deepest consolation? Who knows what might help you when nothing has up to this day? This goes beyond reason. In some parts of Africa and Australia there are similar tribal beliefs in the idea of the Spirit Child. It's as if each unborn baby is a soul plucked from the universe, to inhabit the body of a woman. In some cases that baby is not meant to be born, and so, if something goes wrong, the baby's soul just goes back to the earth, the water, the air, the fire. And then the spirit child waits peacefully for the right time – when it will be born properly. Another mother, another life.

This is what I would do with you, if I were your best friend:

I would go and buy a very pretty little painted box, and invite you to write the name you would have called the baby on a piece of paper, putting it in the box, perhaps with some flowers too. Then I would light two candles, one each side, and tell the baby what you feel, using prayers too, if you wish – and say a heartfelt goodbye. Then take the box and bury or burn it somewhere beautiful, blessing the small soul as it goes on its journey. And after this ritual I would ask you to turn your face towards the light and live at peace with yourself, as your baby would wish.

Two weeks later

AND FINALLY...

Since I wrote about abortion there's been a steady trickle of letters. One or two readers asked me to point out that there are over 170 Pregnancy Crisis Centres in this country that offer post-abortion counselling. (Pregnancy crisis counselling, pregnancy tests and chlamydia tests are also offered.) The post-abortion counselling is free and totally confidential and is a course of about ten weeks. There is also a national helpline called Care Confidential (0800 028 2228 or www.careconfidential.com). Help is offered over the phone and clients can be referred to the nearest centre. In London there is a post-abortion healing course run by Holy Trinity Brompton (email family.life@htb.org.uk, 0845 644 7533).

But Steph's general comment was typical: 'I just felt that I had to write to tell you just how moved I was by your sensitive response to the three ladies who had had abortions. It brought tears to my eyes when reading about the box with the chosen name and a flower to set the spirit of the child free.' Two women wrote to say they'd enacted my suggested ritual:

'Just wanted to send profound thanks for your advice on how to move on from the grief of a termination. It has really helped.' That was S. C., and this was Dawn: 'We named our son on Sunday and followed the suggested ritual. It was the first time my husband had cried about it and I'm sure it will help us to move on as a couple. Thank you so much.'

Yet one reader dissented. Mrs W, a former Pregnancy Advisory Service counsellor, wrote to the paper (not to me personally, which was revealing), sneering, 'I have no idea what qualifies Bel Mooney to give advice … her reply lacked simple common sense and compassion.'

Really? Yet I had carefully explained that I was writing as one who had experienced stillbirth, abortion and miscarriage, and wanted to pass on something that had given consolation to me. One of the world's greatest psychotherapists, Irvin Yalom, writes of 'developing magic rituals to placate' our worst demons. Sometimes these professionals should admit that more imagination is required than patting somebody and saying, 'Never mind.'

White butterfly
Darting among pinks –
whose spirit?

Shiki (nineteenth-century Japanese poet)

3

ADVICE FROM THE PAST

YOU CAN FIND wisdom in unexpected places, including newspapers. In 1937, a pioneering journalist called Eileen Ascroft wrote a weekly 'charm' lesson in the *Daily Mirror*, and went on to set up the first women's page at the *Evening Standard*. Her 'Charm School' columns were collected into a manual called *The Magic Key to Charm*. This was early self-help – and don't forget that advice columns have a long and noble pedigree.

In keeping with the current fashion for nostalgia, this manual has just been republished. Receiving a copy and smiling at the black-and-white pictures of glamorous silky ladies, I thought it would just be dated, harmless fun.

Not so. Old-fashioned it may be, but much timeless common sense in this book would help many of the readers (especially female) who write to this column. Here is one example:

No lipstick can disguise a cruel twist to a mouth, no eye shadow or mascara hides calculating eyes, and no creams or foundations

the lines of discontent and bitterness in a face. The only way to
banish these blemishes is from within.

Who could gainsay that?

The Ascroft idea of 'charm' emphasises the feminine, yet I find much truth in it. Many modern psychotherapists might echo some of her maxims. An essential mixture of self-awareness and selflessness, 'charm' reaches out, aware of the needs of others, yet gaining confidence from self-analysis. Most importantly, it has nothing to do with beauty. It involves good manners, good humour and giving.

To those looking for a partner, she writes:

You cannot find love, but you can help love find you. Stop
seeking and regarding each new man you meet as a possible
husband. Men always sense this … As you learn to develop your
personality you will become much more attractive …
Go about as much as possible, meet new people, make new
friends, travel if you can. Enjoy your life. Go through it with an
air of expectation.

I second that.

This advice was not for bimbos. Eileen suggests learning new words from the dictionary, reading 'a beautiful poem each day' and working through her hefty reading list of classics, as well as going to films and plays and visiting great buildings. Oh yes … make sure you have things to talk about and people will talk to you.

This is as wise as ever.

4

RENUNCIATION

FROM TIME TO time I receive a letter that moves me deeply because of the dignity it displays. These aren't cries for help, but confidences about the human condition. One such came from 'Stephen'. Back in his thirties he married a friend, 'the kindest, sweetest person imaginable'. Now, with three adult children and four grandchildren, he writes, 'Our lives have been very happy and I have total respect for her. I have done my best to be a good husband, father and grandfather, and I always will.'

But, a year ago, at sixty-three, Stephen fell passionately in love with a younger woman. They kissed, that's all – and 'our spirits became as one'. After a while they decided to part completely, since, 'neither of us was prepared to sacrifice the happiness of our respective families'. That was it. A love renounced.

Since then the world has become cold and bleak. There are no longer any colours. I carry on my life from day to day, in sadness, behind a façade of simulated happiness ... Attempting to escape by rationalisation, I listed all the lovely qualities of my wife and the few less desirable qualities of the one I love. Yet I remain totally in love and wonder if I will ever escape from it.

My readers will have, I suspect, widely varying responses. Some people believe you should always follow your heart, on the grounds that we have but one life and a great passion should not be shut out. Others, like Stephen, quail at the thought of destroying the happiness of innocent loved ones. Here is his final paragraph:

I appreciate there is probably nothing you can advise me to do except remain strong. This I will do. I now realise that the condition we call 'Love' knows no boundaries, certainly not of age, and there is much in our lives about which we have much to learn ... My only consolation is my family, and the hope that maybe with the passage of time my feelings will gradually fade and the lovely memories will become shadows, and therefore easier to deal with.

I agree with this sad but noble man that the soul's love can last forever. At the same time, he has surely done the right thing. And – even though it may take a long time – pain does pass.

5

A PROBLEM WITH VISION

I'M TYPING THIS with great difficulty. Just before Christmas I was afflicted by a shadow creeping across one eye. A post-Boxing Day visit to the hospital confirmed that I have a detached retina, and I write not knowing what will happen or whether the operation will be successful. The prognosis isn't that good. I may never regain proper vision in that eye.

So, one minute I'm admiring our beautiful Christmas tree; the next there is this sinister shadow over it. I am always ready to see signs and symbols, and so the sudden shock strikes me as strangely relevant to this role – which forces me to consider the point of view of the reader, and to realise that nothing is crystal clear, no personal angle unimpeded.

People often ask me, when I'm out and about, if the letters on this page are 'real'. I can assure you that every single letter is a genuine cry for help from a real reader, and that if I wanted to write fiction I would return to one of my previous careers as a novelist. And I still write fiction for children, so that impulse is taken care of!

As I've written before, each problem is unique, even if in its essence it is simultaneously universal. There are no new problems under the sun. But so often I want to weep at the partial vision that leads people into emotional cul-de-sacs where they can 'see' only their own point of view. In Shakespeare's great play *King Lear* the Earl of Gloucester, blinded on stage in an act of unimaginable cruelty, subsequently recalls the terrible mistake he has made about his sons and cries out, 'I stumbled when I saw.' And indeed, most of us do too.

My New Year resolution was to carve out more time for peace and relaxation. This problem with my eye may force me to do so. I wish all my readers a Happy New Year, with time for reflection too. Maybe we can all learn from and help each other. With insight.

If you look for the truth outside yourself,
It gets farther and farther away.

Tung-Shan (ninth-century Zen Buddhist)

6

THE LOSS OF A DAUGHTER

Dear Bel,

My beautiful daughter was killed suddenly almost twenty-two years ago, by a drunk driver, on the Sunday evening after a lovely family day. Our family had everything to look forward to. She was my only child. I was looking forward so much to helping her with growing up ... I wish I could talk about Sandra. She would now be almost thirty-three. I loved her and miss her so much and remember her birth, life and death so clearly. The moment she died, and went from my world into another, is indescribable. One blessing is that we shall be together in the same grave. Of course, I will not have grandchildren ... I could write much more but will not do so...

ONCE YOU HAVE experienced such a grief that passes understanding, it flickers around you forever, like a ring of fire. It is a halo of suffering: a crown of burning thorns.

There can be no easy words of consolation for those who have looked into the abyss to see endless sorrow – all their hopes and dreams buried in the darkness. That is why those who have been spared the experience shy away, while those who *know* are able to cross that ring of fire, and hold out a hand. There is a community of suffering.

For many years I have been writing about bereavement; indeed, I made three series of programmes on the subject for Radio 4 and another for BBC2. Yet when I read a letter like yours, I feel lost. Surely no parent will be able to reach the end of your powerful story without feeling tears well up. So please realise how many people are – at this very second – feeling pain on your behalf. You will never meet them but I hope you can tune into that groundswell of sympathy...

At the heart of your letter is this huge question of why people are so lacking in empathy. Even without the experience of bereavement, you would imagine no woman would be so crass as to equate the geographical absence of her son – no doubt a source of unhappiness for her – with such a loss as yours. But people speak without thinking. All of us do...

There is a Latin phrase that crops up repeatedly in medieval literature: *Timor mortis conturbat me*. It means 'The fear of death disturbs me' or, as we might rephrase nowadays, 'Dreading death does my head in.' Think about that in the context of how insensitive people were with you. I've heard stories from bereaved people of how they saw a neighbour actually cross the road to avoid talking to them, or how a dear friend said something as dismissively harsh as, 'You can always have another baby.' We can condemn – or realise, perhaps, that they're merely expressing terror of their own death, of the loss of those they love, of the certain knowledge that, whatever they do, the Grim Reaper will always be there in the next room. One way of dealing with the fear is to dismiss it. Another is to read an article on bereavement (say), then think they understand the so-called 'stages of grief'. It's a way of coping with what terrifies you – to cling to 'answers' like a drowning person clutching at cardboard. As you say, it does not work like that at all.

That grief for the death of a child goes on and on is the experience of wonderful organisations like the Child Death Helpline (www.childdeathhelpline.org.uk, helpline 0800 282 986) and The Compassionate Friends (www.tcf.org.uk, helpline 0845 123 2304). People telephone them many years after their terrible loss, and you should not feel afraid of seeking such help – especially at times like Christmas and birthdays. The Child Bereavement Charity (www.childbereavement.org.uk) is very useful for information on (for example) how men and women grieve differently, and also runs useful discussion forums where people share their grief and find comfort from others who have crossed through the ring of fire.

Can I just say, finally, that you write, 'I wish I could talk about Sandra' – yet you *have* talked to us about her, and I thank you for doing so. Your precious child is (at one remove, but no matter) a part of all our consciousnesses from this day forward – the lesson of her life and death, and your love and grief, absorbed into the lives of people you will never know, who are made better because of it. Such is the community of spiritual awakening. It flies in the face of the *timor mortis*, with the mysterious truth (which you prove) – that love is stronger than death.

One month later

AND FINALLY...

I know readers like to be told about some of those who write to these pages. This instalment involves a coincidence some of you might consider significant.

Four weeks ago, I published a moving letter from 'C' whose only daughter, eleven-year-old Sandra, was killed by a drunk driver twenty-two years ago. Needless to say, her ongoing grief had a profound effect on many readers, whose letters and emails I passed on. Just a week after publishing C's letter I was walking on the sand dunes at Formby, Merseyside – and then wrote about that day here, reflecting how some emotions and experiences are so imprinted on us they last forever.

Now C has written again:

It was amazing to receive the responses from readers. I felt strangely uplifted by all the heartfelt kind thoughts and am sending special thanks to everyone who wrote. I will keep them all. Getting those letters gave me insight into your job and into people – so open and honest. It really does seem to make a real community spirit of mutual interest and help.

Of course, that's exactly how I see this column and it meant a great deal to know we had been useful. C says: 'There is comfort in talking and listening to other people, and realising that we are not really on our own. Many people have dreadful tragedies to bear, and lives much worse than mine.' She tells me that she even had the courage to meet the (elderly) man who had killed her daughter. Sentenced to two years, he had served eight months; he and C talked and she learned that 'his life, to some extent, was ruined too'.

But here's the strangest thing. I had stood by the station bridge at Formby, reminiscing to my husband how, on winter days when I was eleven, my dear dad and I would arrive there to go for our wild walks along the beach. Now I learn that it was on that *exact* spot that C's daughter was killed, at the very age I was in my fond memories. Was it fated that I should be the means of telling Sandra's story?

He who has come through the fire will not fade in the sun.

Hindu proverb

I know your sorrow and I know for the likes of us there is no ease for the heart to be had from words of reason, and that in the very assurance of sorrow fading there is more sorrow. So ... I wish for you ... the strange thing ... that gives us the strength to live on and with our wounds.

Samuel Beckett (Irish novelist and playwright, 1906–89)

7

SECOND-BEST LOVE?

This man wrote to say he was in love with somebody at work. He and his second wife have two children; he feels guilty and asks, 'Do I stay – never be able to give my wife the true love she deserves or do I leave, start again and allow her to find love too?'

As someone who values this precious English language of ours, I have never understood why we persist in cramming a world of complex meaning into one simple little four-letter word: Love. What is love? How many words do the Eskimos have for snow? If we could ban the word 'love' for a month it would force all of us to dig deeply into our feelings and be more precise, more true. 'I'd love that handbag' would have to be rephrased, 'I'd like to see myself with this status accessory on my arm', while 'We loved each other' might be 'translated' as 'We felt a thrilling, forbidden passion for each other.' Your letter states that you love your children, you love your ex-mistress, your wife loves you 'dearly' but you believe your love for her cannot be rekindled. I think we should try to work out what is going on – banishing that lazy little word.

First, let me thank you for your painful honesty. Unlike many men who bluster and seek justification, you start by saying you have 'behaved very badly' and ask for no sympathy. In praising your wife so fulsomely you intensify the feeling of sadness (even indignation) anyone reading your letter must feel, that such a good woman has been deceived and is expending her loyalty and affection on a man who no longer reciprocates. That she is second best in your imagination is a terrible insult to her, even if your confession should be admired at the very least for its frankness. Naturally, I can't help wondering if you left your first wife because you were having an affair with this one. If so, it would throw some light on your personality: one driven by romantic urges at no matter what cost to those around him.

At the moment you feel ground down by family life, disappointed, and full of grief for your lost grand passion. All those feelings are none the less powerful for being very common. No, you are not a monster – just a fallible man who longs for romance and sexual passion. Who knows whether your wife also cherishes such yearnings? In my experience, they are usually part of the rough terrain of married life. So what matters now is how you move on. You say your 'indecision' caused your lady friend to give up on you. Be careful. If you indulge that weak side of your character now you could lose everything and find … no, not another romantic fantasy, but nothing at all.

You have two choices – and one of them isn't to walk out (giving no reason) on those children, for whom you have a deep, powerful affection, or your wife, who is the friend you respect and admire.

Read that sentence again. Think about the feelings it encompasses, then ask yourself if you are prepared to destroy it all because of your (very real) pain at the end of an affair? Are you ready to inflict permanent damage on those boys just because you can't have sex with your colleague any more, and find that (surprise, surprise) marriage lacks 'intensity'? Is making your family 'suffer' (not to mention ending up in a lonely bedsit yourself) better than 'living this lie'? Actually – no, it is not.

I hope you get that new job. In my opinion, you should be strong, stay married, work hard at being a better husband and father, and settle for real life with all its disappointments. But the other choice is this: you confess to your wife what happened, and give her the option of throwing you out. Maybe you'd hope she wouldn't forgive you. But when it came to the point, you may discover that she still thinks you are her 'true' partner for life, and is prepared to live with the fact her first choice has proved to be third rate.

Folly to drink from puddles by the way
When here at home the crystal fountains play!

Angelus Silesius (German priest and poet, 1624–77)

One day you passed before me,
happy and light as air,
and ever since that day,
even without knowing it, I loved you –
with that love which is the very breath
of the universe itself –
mysterious and noble,
both torment and ecstasy of the heart.

Verdi, La traviata (1853)

8

A NEED FOR ROMANCE

THERE I WAS, listening to Verdi's *La traviata* live on Radio 3, thinking about love. We'd just seen Terence Rattigan's play *Deep Blue Sea*, starring Greta Scacchi, at the Theatre Royal Bath. The play is a '50s weepie about a judge's wife who has left her loving, respectable husband for an intensely sexual love affair with a young ex-fighter pilot. From curtain up, their relationship is doomed and at the end Greta/Hester faces ruin alone. Not much romance there. It felt all too true to life for this advice columnist.

Verdi's great opera is about a courtesan, Violetta, who finds true love with a young admirer, Alfredo, but is persuaded to give him up by his father, for the sake of his family's good name. At the end, Violetta is dying of consumption when Alfredo rushes to her side. The music sends your heart soaring, but death parts the lovers for good. And there is nothing romantic about that either.

So then we went to a wonderful party to celebrate 100 years of Mills & Boon publishing. I confess that, over years of writing about human relationships, I've sometimes mocked novels that deceive women into thinking that romance has anything to do with real love and life. Now here I was joining in the celebrations of slushy romance. At the party there were cocktails, champagne and a stall offering pink candy floss, of all things. Then a sweet tenor voice sang 'When I Fall in Love' as gorgeous young guys moved among us giving red roses to the ladies. That perked me up no end.

I learned that a Mills & Boon title is sold every three seconds in the UK and sixty new titles are published every month. My old self would retort that it's because so many gullible women want to be taken in by romance, and are made incapable of facing real life. But now I see the point. While art (*La traviata, Deep Blue Sea* – and any number of great novels like *Anna Karenina*) may leave us uplifted but full of sorrow, Mills & Boon guarantees the longed-for happy ending. And there is a deep human need for that. We cannot help it. So – as the Valentine hearts are hung up for another year – bring on the pink candy floss.

Not to mention young men with roses.

9

A TIME FOR REBIRTH

I LOVE EVERYTHING ABOUT this time of year: the small 'Easter tree' (branch) I decorate with wooden eggs and bunnies, all my family at the table for lunch, the chocolate eggs we exchange – and even the sense that the year has rolled around as it always will, even when I'm no longer here to rejoice at primroses. Tomorrow I shall be sitting in my local church, singing hymns that are in my blood, a part of our heritage. This festival is all about rebirth and, as such, has pagan origins, of course.

Yet there are those who say it's revolting that a religion should have as its central symbol a man tortured on a cross. Can I explain how I see it? The old word for the suffering of Jesus Christ is 'passion', from the Latin verb '*patior*' – 'I suffer'. And it's significant that the word 'patience' derives from it too. There is a philosophical journey within the words. For most of us have no choice but to endure – with whatever patience we can muster – the sorrows of our lives. It doesn't mean we can't try to change things. It just means that instead of moaning 'why me?', we say 'why *not* me?' – and immediately take our places alongside our fellow human beings. When we are able to pity them as *we* wish to be pitied, that fellow feeling is com-passion. Bearing our crosses together – you see?

What helps to carry the cross is faith – in the broadest sense. Those who have a religion can use it to help them, belief in a divine being providing both a structure within which to grieve (God's will) and an external source to shout at (How could you do this, God?). Those of us without that prop can still have faith – but in ourselves, our shared humanity and in the traditions that are our bedrock. For me that includes the symbol of the cross. It reassures me that though life can seem dark and meaningless, redemption lies in our ability to surpass puzzlement, passivity and pain – and be continually reborn into our own lives.

The old (Christian) Blues men expressed the same thought when they sang, from the depths of despair, this faith:

> *Trouble in mind, I'm blue,*
> *But I won't be blue always,*
> *'Cause the sun's gonna shine*
> *In my backdoor someday.*

IO

WHAT IS HOME?

The letter is from a sixty-year-old woman whose husband was unsuccessful in business – with the result that they had to downsize dramatically and she is miserable: 'I did not choose this lifestyle and I feel trapped and very unhappy here, I'm too old and too poor to do anything about it so feel I'm just waiting to die. Do you have any advice to give me?'

WALK ALONG ANY urban road at night and you will glimpse other lives through open curtains – a cosy-looking room here, a bleak one there; a cold, dreary centre light that looks as if nobody bothers much here, a lamp-lit haven there. I love to do that, imagining the lives within. Don't think of me as some kind of snooper, but as a sleuth of the human heart – for our homes do mirror our inner selves.

As somebody for whom 'home' (a big idea – far more than the sum of china and chairs) is hugely important, I have nothing but sympathy as I read how much you miss your old house. But before I go any further, I want you to read the second letter on this page from somebody with cancer who is, indeed, waiting to die. I want you to reflect on the idea of renewal, and reading that letter could be the beginning.

Both letters have grief in common. Of course we cannot equate bereavement nor courage in the face of terminal illness with the forced loss of a garden or a spare room. But your sorrow for the way of life you have lost must not be dismissed by anyone, because it is all too real. The issue is how you can deal with it. There has to be a better way than living with this corrosive self-pity.

You feel that your life has shrunk, and within the smaller space you are forced to confront the terrible inadequacies of your marriage. That is the real problem...

Your letter raises many questions. Why you sensed nothing of your husband's debts. Why he decided to move without your consent and bought this flat you so dislike. At what point in your marriage did you and he give up on talking to each other and considering the other's feelings? Does your husband go to bed so early, worn down by failure – and the knowledge that you despise and resent him for it? Do you know if he misses your former home, but doesn't dare articulate it?

Since I am a year older than you, I will not hear of this 'too old' business! God willing, you have time ahead and so I think you should realise that your husband and you will need each other as a shelter in the years to come. Plenty of people have less than perfect marriages but rub along in a companionable sort of way, realising that when death does come (as it will) being left alone may be the worst thing.

So please – try to talk to your husband about where you are, what you might do. Stop turning your back on him; wake him up. Get that sewing machine out and create a cushion for this man, because he surely needs it as much as you do. You are blessed with family and friends so I think you should talk to them too. Do they know how you feel? Or have they been put off by your (understandable) anger?

The first thing you can do is make this hated flat as pretty a home as possible. In a sunless room a yellow wall works wonders. There's always room for a little IKEA bookcase filled with second-hand books. Get a window-box (or two) to cram with bedding plants. Perhaps persuade your husband to look for a ground-floor flat with a patio or garden. You need to *do* things together. Tell him.

You have wept enough for what's lost. Now is the time to lift your head and work towards a new way of life, in the knowledge that the only en suite that truly matters is the proximity of two people who look out for each other. It's not too late to work on *that* – the real – home.

Everything beckons to us to perceive it,
Murmurs at every turn, 'Remember me!'
A day we passed, too busy to receive it,
Will yet unlock us all its treasury.

Rainer Maria Rilke (Austrian poet, 1875–1926)

II

HOW CAN I LIKE MYSELF?

This 26-year-old teacher says she appears to have 'everything anybody could want' yet does not like herself. 'Do you have any ideas about how I can break out of the morbid, negative cycle of thinking?'

OW DO WE define a full life? A person could be blessed with good looks and good fortune and the love of a good partner, and yet those 'goods' might not combine in the mysterious alchemy that creates happiness. There is so much sorrow in my post-bag; those afflicted by great pain will gnash their teeth wondering why on earth I have picked a letter from a superficially happy person who says she has no real problems. But, as I have said before, life is never so simple. Some heroic people can experience colossal grief and trauma yet rise above them, while others become oppressed by low-level self-criticism, until they are incapable of raising their eyes from the ground beneath their feet. For example, I have here an email from a divorced lady in her fifties, 'Anne', who feels 'aimless and lost' and asks, 'How on earth can I kick-start some sort of inner strength, self-knowledge and self-belief to feel OK about myself?' That question is at the core of your letter too...

Let's seize on the positive aspect of your letter. You say you come into your own when teaching. That's the time when you feel confident – knowing you are good at what you do, presumably because the feedback tells you so. But why is this? When you are teaching, you are forced to believe in yourself as that useful teaching self. There is no time for the inner turmoil that undermines the rest of your life.

You could start by focusing on the qualities that make you a good teacher. It might be useful for you to make a diary of positive thoughts. Each day you need to write down one aspect of your professional day that you know was an achievement. So: 'It was a real breakthrough when Pupil X listened all the way through the lesson without a single silly interruption. Looked engrossed for once!' Follow that with a reason: 'This was because I really did make the topic come alive – and choosing that personal anecdote really fascinated them.' You see?

Divide each page of the diary/notebook in half horizontally. The teaching day comes above the line, but below the line I want you to note down one thing (at least) that is a positive success in your personal life. So: 'I cooked a chicken casserole which Boyfriend said was incredible.' Follow that with a reason. The Negative You might think, 'He's lying again – trying to be nice when I'm a rubbish cook.' But that's not allowed in this special journal. So why else might he have said it? Could it be... 'Because I used fresh herbs and organic chicken this time and I'm really getting better. Thanks Jamie Oliver!' Of course.

Always seek a positive explanation. For instance – did those old friends you dropped not get in touch because they hated you? Of course not. It was because you 'lost' them – and now they're glad you're back on the radar again. Did your colleagues feel 'annoyed' when you left the room? No, they smiled at that witty quip you made. Can you get approval from everybody you meet? No, it's impossible, so don't burden yourself with a futile sense of failure.

It may be that when you were a child people you loved were unduly critical of you, which has left you with this sense of fear. You could spend some time looking back; one day you may even seek proper therapy to find answers. But for now, young as you are, celebrate that woman you see there in the mirror who maybe – just maybe – tries to make life 'nicer' for others because deep down she is a lovely person herself.

People were buying milk, or filling their cars with petrol, or posting letters. And what no one else knew was the appalling weight of the thing they were carrying inside. The superhuman effort it took sometimes to be normal...

Rachel Joyce, *The Unlikely Pilgrimage of Harold Fry* (2012)

12

DAFFODILS

A reader sent me this (shortened) to pass on – something useful drifting
about the web that her sister forwarded from America. It's called 'The
Daffodil Principle', and I don't know who wrote it, though it came with a
picture of the actual place:

S EVERAL TIMES MY daughter had telephoned: 'Mother, you
must come to see the daffodils before they're over.' It was a
two-hour drive. 'I'll come next Tuesday,' I promised on her
third call. Next Tuesday dawned cold and rainy. Reluctantly I drove.
When I finally arrived I was welcomed by my grandchildren. 'Forget
the daffodils, Carolyn! The road's invisible in the fog, and there's
nothing in the world I want to see enough to drive another inch!'

'We're going to see the daffodils,' Carolyn said. 'I'll drive. I'm
used to this.'

After about twenty minutes, we turned onto a small gravel road and I saw a hand-made sign reading, 'Daffodil Garden'. We got out of the car, each took a child's hand, followed the path. Then, as we turned a corner, I looked up and gasped. Before me lay the most glorious sight – as though someone had taken a great vat of gold and poured it over the slopes. Five acres of flowers were planted in great ribbons of deep orange, creamy white and lemon yellow. 'Who did this?' I asked.

'One woman.' Carolyn pointed to a small house sitting in the midst of that glory. We walked up to it. On the patio was a poster saying, 'Answers to the Questions You Are Asking'. The first answer said, '50,000 bulbs.' Then 'One at a time, by one woman.' Then 'Began in 1958.'

That moment was life-changing. I thought of this woman I'd never met, who, more than forty years before, began to bring her vision of beauty and joy to an obscure spot. Planting one bulb at a time, year after year she had forever changed the world in which she lived. One day at a time, she had created something of extraordinary magnificence, beauty and inspiration. The principle her daffodil garden taught is one of celebration. And learning to love the Doing … one step at a time.

'It makes me sad,' I admitted to Carolyn. 'What might I have accomplished if I'd thought of a wonderful goal forty years ago and had worked away at it through all those years? Just think what I might have been able to achieve!'

My daughter summed up the message of the day in her usual direct way. 'Start tomorrow,' she said.

13

RIDING TOWARDS HEALING

Dear Bel,

My mum had me at nineteen, she was beautiful and a lovely mum at first. When I was three, mum and dad divorced and she met a new man. He was violent to her and I started wetting my bed, biting my nails, generally feeling nervous. When I was nine, mum had a baby girl and when I picked her up mum rushed at me, snatched the baby and slapped me across the face. From then on I suffered a catalogue of abuse – like when I wet my knickers and she ripped them off and stuffed them in my mouth, almost suffocating me. Most of the time she acted like she hated me. I felt she was repulsed by me as the 'ugly one'.

I met my future husband when I was seventeen. He loved me unconditionally from the start. We have three sons – my love and my life. But when I had the babies my mum told me I should never expect any help from her. She was in and out of my life, sometimes falling out with me for a year at a time – all for stupid reasons…

I'm forty-three now, with fifteen years of acute anxiety – once housebound for a year. Then I got a bicycle and made myself ride further every day. I still don't go outside my village alone but I can get to most places now if I have a friend with me. I wake most nights feeling frightened and I don't know why. But in the safety of my home I am a warm and loving mum, sing a lot and love being a housewife.

My mum died of cancer last June, aged sixty-two – still very lovely to look at. She hadn't seen me for three years and slagged me off to anyone who'd listen, even telling one of my sons on her deathbed she was sorry he had a mother like me ... I feel sorry for me today as I am grieving for my mum. No pills can ever help me be normal. The GP says he can offer me no more help as cognitive behavioural therapy didn't work and I am a strong person and should get on with it!!! I am falling apart, putting on a lot of weight (comfort eating), feel like I'm choking all the time and can hardly breathe. I go to belly dancing, yoga and swimming once a week and have a little bike ride and walk daily, but still feel ill. Can you suggest anything PLEASE? I trust you as I love your answers and I think I scare my friends as most of them had happy childhoods and good mothers. I've sent you my pic so you know I'm real!!

MAVISxxx

S O REAL – AND smiling out at me from my screen, with your lovely face and curly hair. So real, like *all* those who write to this page and whose letters often make me wonder, week on week, how people can be so stupidly cruel to each other. So very real, all of you, in your will to survive, your extraordinary courage and the loves that keep you going, even when loss makes the horizon bleak and empty indeed. I see your lives as sparks in the vast darkness – and that gives me hope, even when down.

Look at *you*, riding your bicycle so bravely, a bit further each time. You have given us a perfect metaphor for the way people *can* push out the boundaries, despite the odds stacked against them. I want you to go on riding that useful bike towards the sun and hope that it will take you further and further away from the memories of how your mother (and presumably her partner) treated you.

I suggest you are still suffering from a very real grief – not for the woman who was always so vile to you, but for the mother you never had. How can a person ever recover from the anxiety you felt when your mother brought the new man home, the fear you suffered, the rejection you experienced when the baby half-sister supplanted you in your mother's affections, not to mention such abuse? Since your mother was, I suspect, unhappy with her partner by then, she probably projected all her affection on that child – and perhaps you reminded her of the first marriage. Who knows? She died a bitter, unpleasant woman. You may pity her for that, and it would probably also be useful if you can lay the way she treated you to rest by concluding it was due to her own unhappiness. But I wish you would stop thinking of her as 'Mum' and call her 'my mother'. By all means remember her youthful beauty – but she wasn't a 'mum' to you.

She gave you one thing – the determination to be a proper mother in contrast. I want you to start counting your achievements (including those rides) as a way to start forgiving *yourself*. Inside you that rejected child is still crying, believing that this ill-treatment is somehow deserved. But at just seventeen you gained the love of a great guy from a loving family, you have sustained a long and happy marriage, you're a committed mum and the songs you sing express the happiness in your soul that all this is *true*. Please focus on it.

I'm full of admiration for all you've done and are doing. The yoga and swimming and belly dancing are excellent therapies – although you don't want that belly to get too big to shimmy, do you? Please stop comfort eating now, because it will make you feel worse. Don't forget, I can see your lovely face here! Aim to lose the weight you have gained by the anniversary of your mother's death. Then I suggest you do two things on that day. With your husband, light a candle at home telling your mother you hope she is at peace at last, but that she must leave you alone now. Then write her name on a piece of paper, get on your bike and pedal to a lovely spot near where you live in Devon. Do some deep yoga breathing, listen to the birds and look closely at the hedgerow, the grass, the flowers. Meditate on your world. This is real and you deserve its beauty. Then stick the paper in the hedge, or let it blow away on the wind – and go home to your family, blow the candle out, and be well.

Hope is the thing with feathers –
That perches on the soul –
And sings the tune without the words –
And never stops – at all –

Emily Dickinson (American poet, 1830–86)

14

WHAT'S WRONG WITH WOMEN?

This divorced father feels bitter at the way men are treated in general, and in particular that he is 'used' by girlfriends. 'Perhaps you can give me a perspective on where my priorities should lie and if I am unrealistic in expecting women to be less selfish particularly while my children remain dependant on me.'

I T's GOOD YOU read this column every week because you will know it to be even-handed. Unlike some women, I have never subscribed to the 'all men are bastards' prejudice – despite the fact that, very often, some are! For every women abandoned by a husband I can show you a man whose wife has packed her bags. Oh, but *you* know about that side of things, don't you? It's only human to construct a world-view based on our own experience; the danger is that it can be pitifully one-sided.

Now, there will be many readers who agree with your analysis of modern Britain; indeed, I have some sympathy for aspects of your rant. But the politics do not concern me here. You ask rhetorically (about my advice in general) 'What does it all really mean?' Well, of course, mine is necessarily 'a woman's view' but I ask you to understand one important point – which may begin the process of helping you. What the column as a whole 'means', in the most philosophical sense, is beyond gender.

It is about struggling to make sense of things, because one must, but sometimes acknowledging that there are no glib 'answers' – certainly not the sort that politicians and ideologues conjure up to deceive us. It is about pointing out that, sadly, some wounds never heal, therefore one must learn how to tend them so they do not fester. There are some sorrows that will never go away, some grieving you will never get over, some actions with consequences that reverberate forever. You may ask me if I think we are all victims of our fate, with no option but to endure. On one level – yes. Railing against fate never did anyone any good; too often it leads to self-centred bitterness and negativity. But what you can do is muster every ounce of inner strength and accept that none of us can change what has already happened – and then decide to take what you have experienced, absorb what you have learned, and carry it all with you towards the next phase of your life.

Stuck on my dressing table mirror I have a little laminated card. In the autumn of 2003, at a terrible time in my life, it was thrust into my hand at the entrance to the Mission in Carmel. The simple words are from the eighteenth-century founder of the Californian Missions, Father Junípero Serra: 'Always go forward and never turn back.' That's all. So why do I look at it every single day? Because in the beauty and stillness of the Mission garden, by the bronze statue of that long-dead

Franciscan monk, I made a vow to forgive my (then) husband and thus release myself to move forwards into the rest of my precious days, taking with me all the lessons learned through sorrow. Oh yes, and they include an ongoing belief in making allowances, in fairness, in kindness, in trying to understand – and in the ability of the human spirit to remake itself, despite pain. That is what all of *this* 'means'.

Do you think any of the above has anything to do with the sexual equipment we happen to be born with? Of course not. We can't change what has happened but we can change the way we think about what *will* happen – but not unless we stop reading from the sad scripts we have written for ourselves. So, unless you kick your habit of embittered masculine whinging, unless you make a huge effort to stop seeing yourself as a victim of the monstrous regiment of women, you will not be able to find happiness in the future. And there is a more urgent reason for you to change. It worries me that, with two sons, you may be subtly infecting them (a gibe here, a cynical aside there) with your view of women. No good will come of that.

When you go on dates you are carrying all this baggage, and it's bound to put women off. Yes, we can be very selfish, but so can men... Please don't give up. Please don't attribute your unhappiness to some abstract 'ism' – it isn't because of feminism that your marriage fell apart, but because (sadly) people stop loving each other. You're a good dad, but as well as your duty to those boys you have a duty to yourself, to try to be happy. Vow that the next lady you are attracted to won't hear too much about everything that's gone wrong for you. By harping on these things you are being unkind to yourself, and unkindness is catching. Change the script.

The mistake is thinking that the quantity of experiences depends on the circumstances of our life when it depends solely on us ... To two men living the same number of years the world always provides the same sum of experiences. It is up to us to be conscious of them.

Albert Camus (French author and philosopher, 1913–60)

15

GARDENING

'VE NEVER BEEN to the Chelsea Flower Show, but reading about it makes me long to flex green fingers at last. This year my husband and I are determined to make our garden beautiful, with no outside help – except Monty Don & Co., of course. So we've been working away, and as I plant another nemesia or camassia – firming the soil and watering well – I whisper to the plant, begging it not to let me down.

Fifteen years ago, in another house, I tried greenhouse gardening for the first time. My children, unused to seeing me around bags of compost and rocket seeds, mocked: 'Mum's not *gardening!*' so that I felt slightly foolish for having a try. That's the trouble; people who think they know you don't allow you to step outside your previously defined roles. Your fledging confidence dented, you think they may be right, you make a mistake or two, and then it's a short step to giving up altogether. How many people who say, 'I can't cook' or 'We don't garden' are really expressing a fear of failing at what others seem to do so easily?

So be brave – I tell myself. Paint with flowers; edit with secateurs; submit to the daily discipline of weeds. Watching what you have planted thrive (as it will, I hope) is a daily vindication and I believe that a couple who garden together have a good chance of lasting happiness. Even if (as in our case) one does most of the hard work and the other gives advice. I'll leave you to guess which is which…

The news that many people are discovering their gardens again, and responding to increased food prices by planting salads and vegetables on patios and balconies, is very cheering. We're going to try that too. Why not? Imagine if all those who concreted their front lawns for wretched cars had a change of heart. If all school children learned to garden at break time. If willow herb and wild geraniums could carpet our city wastelands and that ancient pagan spirit, the Green Man, triumph again. That's what I dream of when I see those little purple pansy faces telling me it's time to start.

Every place, however small, however seemingly ordinary,
has its own nature.

Russell Page (British garden designer, 1906–85)

16

THE GLUE OF THE UNIVERSE

W E'RE IN THE middle of the Bath International Music
Festival, which is one of the highlights of my year. Every
performance of live music is literally unique: no two
breaths are the same, no pause of exactly the same duration, no
mood identical – and so each time the work is made anew. In recent
years the Bath Music Festival has evolved from strictly classical
(when I started attending in 1981) to a cornucopia of styles: jazz
experimental, world, gospel, folk, blues, as well as the classical rep-
ertoire, which remains the backbone. I sup it all up like champagne.

That's why I hate the musical apartheid of our times. My daughter
used to love a great movie called *Empire Records* with its catchphrase,
'Music is the glue of the universe.' Yet how can that be true if people
don't listen to each other's sounds? When the Bath Festival pushed
out boundaries, the old school moaned: to them only classical music
was 'proper'. On the other side, there are all those narrow-minded
people who call classical music and opera 'highbrow'. What non-
sense. Mozart and Puccini were once 'pop' – meaning popular.

Once children listened to nursery rhymes, novelty songs and lots of classical music too; at my Liverpool primary school in the '50s we sang a beautiful song by Handel: 'Did you not hear my lady, go down the garden singing.' Now they binge on non-stop pop. If only the unhappy teenagers who write to me were to listen to Albinoni's 'Adagio' or a Chopin Nocturne, they might find their moods expressed to perfection. Great music can heal – whether it's by Bach or Burt Bacharach.

A week ago we were thrilled by a mind-blowing concert in Bath given by trumpet virtuoso Alison Balsom and her ensemble. You have to imagine a stunning blonde, more sexy than any model but dressed just like one, playing Vivaldi, Handel and Purcell with such *brio* I wanted to dance. It was amazing. Everyone should see her at least once in their lives.

So here's my advice for everyone this week. Listen to somebody else's music and make it yours. Alternate Gregorian chant with music from Mali. Break your heart with Amal Murkus's Palestinian songs or Rachmaninov. Kids – listen to the conversation between piano and cello in Beethoven's 'Spring'. Oldies – get the poetry of 'Never Went to Church' by The Streets. Let's stick the fragmented universe together.

To know what is going on takes sense.
To know what to do about it takes wisdom.

Old Chinese proverb

17

THE PITH OF IT

NOT MUSIC BUT marriage this week – but the way in is music once again. At the Bath Music Festival we saw the brilliant American guitarist Bob Brozman and bought his funky new CD: *Post-Industrial Blues*. Now, I'm one of those nerdy people who reads every word of sleeve notes and that was how, in the small hours of the morning, I found these words by Brozman in tiny print:

The creative work I have been able to do with my wife Haley goes hand in hand with our passionate way of being around the world. Our life together is one long and inspiring brainstorming session that is full of ideas, humour, passion and tenderness. I hope the listener can feel some of this in the music. It is always dedicated to her.

I found that exhilarating and inspiring: worth holding up as an ideal for newly married couples (you can substitute 'seriously cohabiting' if you like) to keep in mind – as well as giving longer-marrieds food for thought. Now obviously this is a lucky couple who can travel together and are involved in a fascinating business – but no matter. Bob Brozman's four nouns can be the four corners of anybody's relationship, holding it steady.

Ideas keep you talking, sharing, discovering. *Humour* stops you taking yourself too seriously and every couple needs silly private jokes. *Passion* is easy at first but harder to sustain, unless you see that it doesn't have to involve hot sex five times a week, but warmth and love, and also a passion for similar things. *Tenderness* is almost the most important one of all – the mutual caring that will take you through the most difficult times. Commit them to memory and see how you can work to keep them alive in your own life. To help you remember the four tenets, rearrange the initial letters (so it goes Passion, Ideas, Tenderness and Humour) and you have the acronym PITH.

That's even more useful because one of the definitions of 'pith' is: 'The central or most important part of something.' And even when your passions and your ideas start to fade, tenderness and humour will see you through right until the end.

18

HOW DO YOU CHANGE?

Dear Bel,

I'm forty-eight, my partner C is forty and we've known each other for three years. I'd be grateful if you could tell us how to change our lives. We are sick of what we have. Every day the same old drudge, mess and misery...

I have a job stacking supermarket shelves for miserable money. I'm in debt and rely on C to feed and clothe me as she can earn double what I earn – but it still won't get us where we want to be ... I want to move on in life ... yet here I am, still alive, doing nothing. I need someone who can show me how to get on in life. I have spent years following the advice of self-help books but it all remains the same...

I can't accept my lot in life. I dream of being a wedding photographer and going on a course to learn the trade, but how – without money or a car? People say, 'Only you can help yourself.' But I've tried everything I can think of: tarot cards, wishful thinking, visualisation techniques, books, friends,

Samaritans, prayer spells (to try to lift the curse). I believe there is a latent force at work making sure I live the life I have. But why? I refuse to waste my life away in a dead-end job, knowing it's not enough to put food on the table. I don't want another job – the chances are it would be a day job – less money and little time for photography. I don't want your shoulder to cry on. Both C and myself have cried enough tears of frustration and we don't want to whinge on about how unfair life is. All we want is a chance – just tell us what we must do to get fate off our backs. We need money to let us lead the life we want. We want to get married with a proper church wedding, to travel, to get the photography up and running ... If there is a way to change our lives, why can't we see it?

Chris

YOU MAY NOT want a shoulder, but you have one. Your letter haunted me while I read a magazine feature about what was spent on four spoilt rich girls' sixteenth birthdays by parents with more money than wisdom, judgement or taste. Here's a monstrously selfish brat getting the £16,995 sports car she demanded when she can't yet drive – and there is a decent 48-year-old man desperate for a break in life. It's enough to turn you into a revolutionary.

Yet, I've never been one because I'm a realist – and all the wishing in the world will not deliver equality this side of heaven. You list various sources you've consulted in your search for a way to change your life for the better and tell me none has worked. So I need to try a different tack, but with a warning. You may find what I have to say tough – and therefore I repeat how much I genuinely sympathise with your predicament.

With frustration you quote, 'Only you can help yourself' and ask how on earth to start. You're right: self-sufficiency is limited. Many people just need a leg-up: that helping hand, that inspirational coach, that business loan, that offer of training. Yet at the same time, the mindset has to be such that you actively seek the help. I've read your letter about six times and can only conclude that, with all this terrible defeatist talk of a 'latent force' and a 'curse', you *have* to change your outlook.

First, I must point out that all those who have made academic studies of happiness (at least nine volumes on my shelf) will tell you that you start from the biggest advantage: your loving relationship. Despite all the pain each of you has suffered, you and C have found your soulmate. This is the basis from which you begin your quest – and I just want you to pause and give thanks for that.

Second, I want to pour water on the 'Just follow your dream' philosophy, which deceives people into the belief that dreaming will deliver. It won't. Yes, have a goal in life – but who would counsel following a dream if the fantasy leads you into a bog you get stuck in? So, because you can't attain the dream, you do nothing at all. That's what has happened with you. What if I were to suggest you ditch this idea of becoming a wedding photographer? Your letter is written in capitals on file paper: you have no computer skills, which are as necessary as a love of taking pictures. Modern wedding photography is a slick, hard business (there's dozens in your area – I looked) and photography in general is a tough way to earn any sort of living. Will it surprise you to know that many wannabe snappers don't make even as much *regular* money as you do? I think you should keep it as an enjoyable hobby, check out competitions and go for it (take moody night-time pics at work) and in the meantime move on from dreams to practicalities.

Readers may be bothered by something in your letter. You weep because you're in a dead-end job yet say you 'don't want another job' because 'the chances are ... etc.' What? You're stacking shelves nights and haven't even investigated whether you could get a better job? Chris, if you want to change your life and make more money, that simply isn't good enough. I know a wonderful woman in her forties who stacks shelves yet gets up off the couch (she won't allow herself to get into bed in case the sleep is too deep) a few hours later and goes and cleans houses with good cheer to feed her two teens. I know another man who advertises himself as 'No Job Too Small' and makes a living doing odd jobs. Be energised. Why didn't that pesky tarot reader tell you to *act*? Have you investigated skills training in your area? Go to the Citizens Advice Bureau and see what they suggest about (a) your debt and (b) your lack of skills.

You are C's new family. Show her how much you love her by taking a lead, one step at a time. And please set a date for that wedding. By all means go for the church if you have sincere religious faith but if not, what are you waiting for? A registry office does the job, and you don't need to save up. The more you ask how far it is, the longer your journey seems. The more you weep for what you haven't got, the more you will be blinded to possibility.

Two weeks later

AND FINALLY...

When poor Chris wrote about his frustration stacking shelves, longing to be a photographer and having no money, I expected readers to respond. Most were slightly frustrated with him. But there was a helpful suggestion that he could start with cut-price weddings and portraits if he is really serious about photography. No matter – I want to share two responses showing inspirational strength of character.

Sue, from Maldon, Essex, writes:

Me and my husband both stack shelves for a living and it's hard to make ends meet. We are both in our forties. I have recovered (hooray) from breast cancer and my husband has epilepsy, which is under control. The best thing in our lives is our strong love for each other. You're right to tell Chris to get his debt sorted out. I know it's hard but if you put a little aside each month you can save for what you need. You don't need to spend a lot on a wedding. We didn't. A register office is fine. My dad drove. My sister took photos. My friend made the cake. We had a happy day and that's what's important.

There's blessings counted for you.

Then Beverly asks, 'How can his life be full of "drudge, mess and misery" each day when he wakes up next to someone he loves to bits?' and says she would love to find somebody like that. The father of her two girls left ten years ago; she has brought them up alone, 'one with physical disabilities in a wheelchair, the other with "hidden" disabilities: visual/special problems and mild learning difficulties'. Beverly says her first daughter (studying for A levels now) has never complained: 'I used to watch her sometimes when other children were playing and there was never any envy in her gaze but a rapt attention – she was dancing and running with them in her imagination.'

She goes on:

I refuse to become downtrodden so constantly seek new ways to improve their lives, and mine too. You don't have to look too hard to see people who are infinitely worse off and equally those better off too. I detect a note of envy in Chris which is corroding to the spirit. With optimism and hope he could achieve so much.

I cannot add to that wisdom.

We do not see things as they are, we see them as we are.

Talmud (Jewish religious law)

19

BAD KARMA

This was a distressing letter from a 62-year-old who was abused by her father. She asked: 'Do you think that we suffer in this life because of something bad we have done in a previous life? I know some people believe we are climbing spiritual levels, but I am an atheist because I cannot believe in a God who would let little children suffer so, and I also feel that, if we did something bad in a previous life, we should be punished in that life, not this.'

THOSE WHO WRITE about human feelings and relationships realise the limitations of words, which sometimes seem to teeter on the brink of an abyss containing impenetrable darkness. Sometimes the howls from that black hole threaten to drown out all reason, all attempts at consolation. Still, we must try. Therefore, I begin with a wordless hug, spirit to spirit, because we shall never meet. You will have awakened that impulse in many who will share my horror at what you have endured...

Would that your vile father had left before you were two. What happened to you is monstrous. I wish the medieval images of hell I have seen in European churches are a true vision and that man is being tortured by demons forever. Many will say that if you could somehow forgive him you might find inner peace, but I cannot write that (even though I suspect it's true) because I don't feel it. You have every right to feel angry at the way your whole life was polluted; the extent of his legacy of misery and pain.

You are also entitled to feel jealous of happy childhoods. Please don't flagellate yourself with the description, 'cold and selfish'. Listen to Rabbi Harold S. Kushner, writing in his classic bestseller, *When Bad Things Happen to Good People*:

> *…being angry at the situation, recognising it as something rotten, unfair and totally undeserved, shouting about it, denouncing it, crying over it, permits us to discharge the anger which is part of being hurt, without making it harder for us to be helped. Jealousy is almost as inevitable a part of being hurt by life as are guilt and anger. How can the injured person not feel jealous of people who may not deserve better, but who have received better?*

Your question about belief splits into two because reincarnation is not part of the central Christian tradition. You say you're an atheist because you don't believe in a God who lets children suffer. The problem of pain has preoccupied thinkers and theologians for centuries, and none of the scores of books on my shelves comes up with one answer. A parent whose child was the victim of an Ian Brady or Fred West may scream out your question, but so will one whose child was killed by a car. To accept the entirely random nature of fate is, I suppose, a way of dealing with this. It's my own method. Personally, I do not believe in reincarnation, although I have no more proof that I won't come back as a shark than I have of paradise as a reward. Many faiths (not just Hinduism) and systems of thought discuss the possibility of rebirth; it is clearly an essential human preoccupation, perhaps founded upon our reluctance to accept the finality of death. Myself, I believe in one life, and making the most of it. But I also believe in developing a spiritual sense while alive. Many of us talk about good and bad karma, don't we?

You're a thoughtful woman; I hope you have sought therapy to help you deal with your own demons. If not, I do urge it, as it would certainly do you good to talk to somebody qualified. In the meantime, I refuse to believe there is no hope in this story, so ask you to start by giving yourself credit for the way you arrested your alcoholism. Your poor mother believed you and sought to protect you in the end. You married a 'good' man. You've mended your relationships with a family that has stood by you, no matter what. You are *loved*, Shirley.

Let us suppose you have thirty years left now (why not? I hope I do) in which to cherish a life you can rejoice in. Think of that life as something infinitely precious you hold in your hand, which nobody can touch, certainly not that brutal ghost. Going on as you have already begun – with amazing courage – is the best method of exorcism.

*Forgiveness is as valuable to the one who forgives
as to the one forgiven.*

Mary Witcher (nineteenth-century American Shaker)

20

FORGIVE THE PENITENT (1)

This young man (twenty-five) will not forgive his mother for running off
with another man and hasn't spoken to her for four years, despite her pleas.
The marriage had not been good, but the father did his best to turn his two
sons against their errant mother. Now the writer is in love and his girlfriend
became upset to read a card from his mother: 'I can understand Chrissie's
reaction to a certain degree, especially as her mother died when she was
thirteen. But rightly or wrongly, surely she has to accept that this is my
choice and that there is a matter of principle here?'

S OMEBODY ONCE SAID that whenever two good people argue
over a principle they are both right. And experience tells me
that when a person as young as you are talks so rigidly about
sticking to a principle, there's a real danger of getting well and truly
stuck. Call me unprincipled, if you like, but I never learned to value
a principle that caused misery.

After that preamble, you know what I am going to say. You predicted I'd come out in solidarity with the 'fallen' penitent mother you have rejected. So why did you write? I suspect that deep down you know that you have to start learning to forgive your mother. But you had no need to consult a stranger. The lovely girl at your side is the one you should listen to.

Let me make it clear that I do understand why you were so angry with your mother for breaking up the family. People always underestimate the effect of a divorce on grown children, and they shouldn't. How a separation is handled can have a profound effect on the future wellbeing of the young people involved – and any children they might have. You and your brother went through a tough time, and your response was to slam the door on the person who caused it. Who dares say you weren't 'right' at that time?

Yet your father was not an innocent, but difficult and selfish. You do not know what went on between them, nor how unhappy your mother became. He took advantage of your shock and rage to make you judge, jury and executioner on this woman who gave birth to you and your brother. Is that fair? I repeat – you *cannot* know the complexities of their marriage, even though you realised all was not smooth.

On the other hand, what does Chrissie know? That she would dearly love her own mother to be alive and able to witness the rest of her life. That the man she loves has already lied to her. That he thinks his judgement on his mother is none of her business and she should accept his decision without question. Oh dear. Are you telling me you want to spend the rest of your life with this girl whose feelings and wise judgement you are prepared to ignore? Are you sure she'll want to share her future with a guy so difficult and selfish that he's already telling her he doesn't care what she thinks?

This resentment must stop in order to enable you to move towards your future with this person you love. Thank goodness you're young enough to change – for if you don't, your happiness is in jeopardy. Naturally, Chrissie wants to meet your mother and so you must demonstrate your love and respect for her (whatever you feel about your mum) by making this happen. First, you should talk to your brother, find out the state of their relationship, and ask him to help you set up a meeting. I think it will be best for you to meet her with him, to dilute the encounter. Later you will introduce her to your girlfriend.

For the woman you love is saying this: 'When people are dead you miss them forever, so please forgive her so that maybe I can have a relationship with a mum figure and when we have children she can be a loving granny – and anyway, my darling, bitterness will just dry you up inside…'

So you have no choice but to listen.

To her, not me.

Forgiveness is giving up all hope of having had a better past.

Anne Lamott (American novelist, b. 1954)

21

HANDS-ON DAD

FATHER'S DAY IS often dismissed as a commercial construct, but surely it makes us celebrate a vital figure? If possible, families *do* need caring fathers, who should cherish their unique role. To define a good dad I can only invoke my own childhood, sharing some of the parenting lessons I learned at Ted Mooney's knee.

He was There. Always There.

He *knew* stuff because he went to the library. And he laughed a lot as well.

He worked all the hours he could at the English Electric Company and then studied as many hours to get a valuable Higher National Certificate to give his family a better life. His example was hard work and possibility.

He'd take us to the cartoon theatre on Saturdays and recognised the importance of slurping an Orange Maid – and the weekly *Dandy* and *Beano* too.

He knew that if you couldn't afford holidays the kids needed
   bucket-and-spade days out, and he'd never be too busy for that.

When the thunder and lightning cracked over the flats, he knew
   to come in and tell me softly it was only the clouds bumping
   together.

When the nightmare terrified me into yelling, 'Daaaaaad!!!!' he
   was there in seconds, never saying 'Don't be silly' and knowing
   how to tuck me in *so* tight (this before duvets) nothing nasty
   could get into the bed.

When we were little he polished our leather shoes (winter) and
   sandals (summer) to a shine every night, because appearances
   matter.

He redecorated the flat every year, demonstrating how to take a
   pride in where you live, even if you don't actually own it.

When it was windy and rainy he'd say, 'Shall we go on the ferry?'
   and the two of us would take the bus to the Pier Head and wrap
   up on the deck looking back at the lights of Liverpool – and so
   he made wind and rain an adventure.

And so on. Thank God there are still hands-on fathers who fit the
mood of that, putting their families first. I salute them – and my own.

22

A GOOD MAN

Here's a lady whose first husband left her and their daughters for another woman. She then married a man who had also been left but became a good stepfather. Now he's fifty-five and she's restless: 'He is intelligent but poorly educated; I'm disappointed that he rarely reads a book or listens to Radio 4. He loves dancing, walking, gardening and bird-watching – all of which we enjoy together. So am I being unreasonable in wanting to have discussions about politics and books? ... How can I make the best of my situation when I feel so angry with myself?'

AVING READ YOUR long, unhappy letter three times before editing it for the page, I find myself more confused as to why you feel so angry with yourself. At the same time, I confess to a frisson of irritation because – oh, fortunate woman – you simply do not realise how lucky you are. You believe you've made mistakes all your life. Therefore, it's my duty to point out, quite firmly, that you run a very real risk of making the biggest one of the lot...

Reaching middle age, many people suffer what T. S. Eliot described as, 'the rending pain of re-enactment / Of all that you have done, and been...' It is negative and bleak. Only you can begin to reflect on your life and look back into childhood, asking where your dislike of yourself began, setting a pattern for future behaviour. Did a parent put you down? Did some early hurt stick like a thorn, over which your skin closed, never to heal properly? I see a destructive circle where you continually feel you aren't worthy of something/someone (university/your first husband) then act as if that feeling were true – and therefore it becomes true, with dire consequences. The irony now is that you have found a man who – over and over again – has proved himself to be worthy of you, and yet you are telling me you doubt it – citing piddling 'reasons' like not liking Radio 4...

No, the truth is far more complicated. You do not believe you are loveable, yet saw how this excellent man loved you, moved away from his family to be a wonderful stepfather to your girls, supported your retraining, shares lots of interests with you and wants nothing more than to live contentedly looking after you and your home. Deep down you can't respect someone who loves imperfect *you* like that, and so you seek to diminish him. Angry with yourself for not being worthy of love, you transfer that anger to him and his perceived lack of scintillating 'dinner party conversation'. If you only knew how many women reading this would give anything to be married to a caring man like yours. Do yourself a favour and make a little list of all the uncaring things your first husband did – and, for pity's sake, stop romanticising that man.

As someone who has sat through countless dinner parties in my time, surrounded by over-achievers interminably wrangling about sterile politics, let me tell you how idyllic your life sounds. Bird-watching and gardening and pottering, eh? To stroll hand in hand towards old age, whiling away peaceful hours in such pursuits sounds blissful to me. I have a favourite quotation from Michael Cunningham's book *The Hours*: 'These days, Clarissa believes, you measure people first by their kindness and their capacity for devotion. You get tired, sometimes, of wit and intellect; everybody's little displays of genius.'

Are you terrified of ageing? You seem to be consuming yourself in futile wishes, unable to cope with the realities of the everyday. Parents will get old and require our care, children will grow, leave home and require less of it: becoming a whole, mature human being involves acceptance of these realities, as well as acknowledging that we will never 'be free'. Wistfully requiring so much, you are doomed to perpetual disappointment. If you waste your life being angry with the universe for not delivering perfection, it will be impossible for you ever to feel at peace with yourself.

'Count your blessings' may be sound advice, but it is rarely appreciated. You know how important it is because you say you 'try very hard to be grateful'. At fifty you have (God willing) many years ahead of you, so I beg you to stop this hysterical self-blame and congratulate yourself for earning the love of this patient man. You did not marry him 'on the rebound', but after three whole years, and you've both survived much pain to reach this middle age of co-existence. Don't spoil it. Dance with him. And realise that there is as much glory in a kingfisher's feathers as in a whole shelf of books.

A few weeks later

AND FINALLY...

The letter from 'K', discontented with her 'poorly educated' second husband, prompted 'S' to write sadly, 'I can totally empathise as I too have turned fifty and for the past three years have felt dissatisfied with my marriage of twenty-eight years.' 'C' wrote:

I am a typical fifty-year-old female, with a good-natured but dull husband who comes under more scrutiny than his placid personality can bear. With both kids at uni he now gets the full force of my (menopausal?) frustrations and his shortcomings seem magnified. I often think, can I stand another twenty to thirty years of the banalities of our everyday life?

But others were irritated with 'K'. Elizabeth wrote movingly:

Does this woman not realise what she has? My beautiful man died in July after twenty-eight years ... Pete never read a book, wasn't political, but the legacy of love he left behind is immeasurable ... His gentleness in an ever more violent world ... The beauty in a piece of wood he made into a box. I earned far more than Pete, was more ambitious and had my finger on the pulse. But who was the more content, more peaceful, and defiantly more full of love and joy? He bought me white daisies every week. Said we were cosy. What I would give to have that 'cosy' again.

Is it mere luck that makes a good marriage? Or tolerance as well as hard work? Whatever the alchemy, it's always uplifting to be reminded of long-lasting love. Last Saturday we took my parents up to Liverpool for a surprise sixty-fifth birthday bash my cousin Gina had arranged for her husband Mike. In his touching speech he said, 'I've been married to Gina for forty-one years and still love her as much today as I did then.' I remembered their wedding, when Mike was a mop-top who'd jammed with George Harrison and she a beauty (still is!) who'd dated pre-Beatles Ringo. And there they were, dancing with their grandchildren. No wonder reader Annabel Cope has these words stuck up all over her house: 'Life may not be the party that we hoped for, but while we're here we might as well dance.'

Gold becomes consistently more beautiful with
every blow inflicted by the jeweller's hand.

Rumi (Persian poet and mystic, 1207–73)

It isn't for the moment you are struck that you need courage. But for the long uphill climb back to sanity and faith and security.

Anne Morrow Lindbergh (American author, 1906–2010)

23

STILL MOURNING

A young woman's fiancé died in a car crash nine years ago and now she cannot form a new relationship, although she has tried: 'But it doesn't take much to bring tears to my eyes when I think or talk about him. After nine years, surely this isn't right? How can I explain why his death is still having such an impact on my life? How can I get over this and start living normally? I really don't know and don't know who to ask.'

WHAT IS A 'normal' life? I sometimes think that people can waste away inside with wishing for the impossible dream of a so-called normal – or ordinary – life. I believe that all lives are extraordinary, and if each of us released ourselves into that realisation, the world would be a richer, more fulfilled place. I look at people on the street – normal, ordinary folk going about their business (probably feeling down because of the rotten summer) and see complicated bundles of emotions, most of them hidden from the world around. I see loss and longing, jealousy and joy, dread and delight – in the most 'normal' people, most of whom manage to hide their feelings, just as you hide your ongoing pain. So first I want you to stop thinking of yourself as some kind of freak, and understand that just as every soul is extraordinary in its own way, so there is no regimented timetable for emotions.

I do not believe that we ever 'get over' a bereavement – in the sense of entirely leaving it behind, making a new start, moving on, or any other helpful phrase. You cannot leave behind any experience that has had a profound effect on the shape of your life, and a 'new start' cannot be put on like a mask. Surely we are each the sum total of everything that has happened to us? Therefore, I believe we carry our sorrows with us, just as a snowball, rolling down the hill, picks up snow as it goes. Do you think that sounds gloomy? On the contrary, I intend it as robustly encouraging – because the snowball is, at the end of its journey, much bigger than when it started its roll forward. And seeing ourselves as becoming larger through experience is cause for quiet celebration.

All that is to suggest to you that you are allowed to feel what you feel for as long as you like. The other week I was telling a wonderful doctor my medical history, mentioned having a stillborn son and naturally my voice wobbled and my eyes filled with tears – thirty-three years on. Grief does not go away – why should it? Yet it *does* change, to become absorbed into life, changing one forever.

Around the same time as your letter, I received one from Sue (forty-five) who had just endured the cruel experience of being on holiday with her sixty-year-old fiancé (an acquaintance of nineteen years' standing, but new love, three years after he became a widower) when he died of a pulmonary embolism. That was in April and they were to have married on 27 September. She writes, 'I just don't know what to do with myself. Life has no purpose or meaning now if he is not with me. Where do I go from here? I am floundering without him. I weep and weep for his loss.'

There are no glib words to console Sue, four months after fate suddenly snatched her love away – nor for you, nine years on. Both of you experienced loss made worse by its suddenness – and also, perhaps, by the complications and difficulties that were an inherent part of the immediate past. All I want you to know is that whenever I write about bereavement, readers get in touch with words of sympathy, saying they had tears in their eyes, and perhaps were reminded of their own losses. Of course you are right to say that people get on with their own lives and can't be expected (say) to recall the anniversary of your beloved's death. Yet people *do* understand. And when the world seems meaningless, it can be helpful to realise that 'meaning' lies in the sympathy of others, as well as the strength we can summon to walk through the valley of shadows.

I calculate you are about eight years younger than Sue, yet nine years older in experience of grief. So what would you tell her? I imagine you would suggest counselling, since you found it helpful – and probably should consider it again to help you now. You will, I'm sure, also hold out an imaginary hand, saying you know that grief can be borne – even if with difficulty. Sue asks, 'Where do I go from here?' and my answer to you both is – onwards. In the knowledge that having experienced great love once, you are transformed forever by its grace. Who knows what use you may make of it in time, or how it may lead you to fresh happiness?

I grumbled because I had no shoes
until I met a man with no feet.

Chinese proverb

24

PROVIDENCE

EXACTLY A WEEK ago I had an experience of beauty and harmony that will last my lifetime. Fittingly, it was on the last night of our New England trip and we were in a formerly run-down city called Providence, in America's smallest state, Rhode Island.

We'd been told about the famous event called WaterFire – which consists of a whole lot of braziers lit along the middle of the river and music playing and people hanging out on the streets… 'Sounds quite fun,' I thought. Nothing prepared me for a powerful work of art – a living ritual in which fire, water, sound and smell all play a part to reduce you to awestruck silence and (in my case) tears of joy. And all for free. This celebration of renewal takes place regularly through summer and autumn. On the day of a WaterFire event volunteers begin at 6 a.m., setting a hundred fires in braziers strung like a necklace along the river. Speakers are hung from the sides, extra lighting provided in dark underpasses, and so on. There is no room here to describe the complexity of this regular installation but you can find out more at www.waterfire.org.

At sunset, the streets are thronged: all ages, all races, all 'types'. A gong is struck, and the braziers lit in turn. At the same time, the music starts, no piece lasting more than about five minutes, and ranging from folksong, through classical, to world and 'new age' – but all haunting and uplifting. It all goes on until after midnight. We took a boat along the fires, breathing the sweet scent of cedar and gazing up at the faces of the thousands watching WaterFire. This was when it hit me. There was such quiet delight in those crowds: no rowdiness, no squawks of derision when opera suddenly floated across the water, no shrieking drunks (no alcohol allowed except in a designated food area). The people rose to the magic of the event. Which proves my innate belief that the best is *possible*.

I'm a great believer in giving thanks when something wonderful happens. Sometimes I thank God, sometimes the universe – but that night, for the first time, I could (literally) thank Providence.

Sometimes things don't go, after all,
from bad to worse. Some years muscadel
faces down frost; green thrives; the crops don't fail.
Sometimes a man aims high and all goes well.

Sheenagh Pugh (British poet and novelist, b. 1950)

25

A LITTLE HELP FROM MY FRIENDS

ASKED TO SPEAK at a 'Forty Years On' reunion at University College London, I said yes – though never before interested in such nostalgia. There we all were – those bright young things who had bought the brand new LP, *Sgt Pepper's Lonely Hearts Club Band*, listened to pirate radio stations, demonstrated against the Vietnam War, felt grief and outrage at the murder of Martin Luther King, marvelled at the first men on the moon and danced to Pink Floyd at the UCL hop… 'Ah, yes, I remember it well.' This disparate group of strangers toured the truly magnificent building, with ornate stucco, which we were too callow to notice in those far-off days. We murmured that this bit was new but that was the same … and all of us wondering where the time had gone.

You know how it is. One minute you're a funky, rebellious chick in a mini skirt and then, in the blink of an eye, you've morphed into a 62-year-old pillar of society. One minute you're growing long hair and a Zapata moustache and then, in an intake of breath, you're grey and worried about retirement. In between there were the love affairs, jobs, children, marriages ('Will you still need me? Will you still please me?'), divorces, bereavements, money worries – all the joy, all the pain. One minute you have your life before you and then, in the beat of a heart, you're forced to contemplate old age and death.

We had a good day and my speech raised some smiles – as well as pride in the old passions of my generation. I think we all felt lucky to be students forty years ago, when there were plenty of jobs and no student debt and it really did seem to be 'getting better all the time'. But I realised why, as you get older, nostalgia is inevitable. It briefly stops the passage of time. Contemplating who you were, what you believed in, you realise that the essence of that person has changed as little as the sculptures and paintings that grace the old college. As I told an appreciative, understanding audience of baby boomers, despite 'the news today, oh boy', I still believe in Peace and Love, and want to go on working towards it… 'With a little help from my friends.' It's the only way to 'get by' without becoming melancholy.

At dawn I sighed to see my hairs fall,
At dusk I sighed to see my hairs fall,
For I dreaded the time when the last lock should go…
They are all gone and I do not mind at all!
I have done with all that cumbrous washing and getting dry…

Po Chü-i (eighth-century Chinese poet)

26

FORGIVE THE PENITENT (2)

Dear Bel,

Some months ago a young man wrote for advice regarding his mother
who had left his father. He felt he didn't want ever to have a relationship
with her. I was convinced that one of my sons had written the letter as the
circumstances were almost identical. You gave such sound and caring advice
I hoped I might hear from him ... My ex-husband is still living in the house
with both of my sons and has been threatened with imprisonment and will
be evicted and the house will be sold if he refuses to co-operate with the
court ... The disapproval I received from my sons was understandable and I
accept that my behaviour at the time gave them every reason to be angry
but now not only am I an adulterer and a bad mother, but am also condemned
as an evil money-grabbing bitch who is relishing the thought of making her
family homeless ... It's not only me they have rejected but everyone in my
family, including my 87-year-old father, who has all but given up hope of
seeing his beloved grandsons again.

T HAT LETTER WAS not from one of your sons, although you are right to see the coincidences as extraordinary. As Shakespeare knew, there are only so many plots within the human condition. He himself borrowed from the great myths that continue to throw light on the repetitive problems of humankind. Love, infidelity, retribution … it goes on and on, in great cycles of unhappiness. An unfaithful mother who connives with her lover to kill her husband, only to be killed herself in retribution by a son who is then doomed to suffer for that act – that's one of the great stories of Greek tragedy. And being played out today, in your life.

Let me explain – before you protest indignantly that you have not 'killed' your husband. When one spouse leaves a partnership against the will of the other, extreme violence is done to that marriage. Something is destroyed – and all the pussyfooting justification in the world will not alter that truth – or children will be hurt, no matter what age they are. Small children may forgive; young people in their twenties are likely to become set in resentment, especially if the wronged spouse pours poison in their ears. Thus have your sons determined to punish you – even if (as I wrote to that first young man) it is likely to doom them to even more unhappiness in the long term.

There are two themes within your letter that we should disentangle before trying to find a way forward. First there was your decision to leave home because you had fallen in love with somebody else. Then came your choice to go for a 50/50 split (your right in law, but not necessarily within the moral universe) on the home your husband and sons share. You acted first from love, then money.

Your sons will have seen the legal action as the last straw. It's a sad situation; you are all in a stalemate while the lawyers are making money.

Let's jump to the plight of the 87-year-old grandfather who longs to see his grandsons again. These men are not children and must realise that whatever the damage for which they blame their mother, there is no justice in punishing an old man who has done them no harm at all. If they're reading this, I would add that only the gravest wrongs within a family are actually 'unforgivable'. They will never be able to understand the complexity of what went on between you and your husband, or to what extent his behaviour drove you to the arms of another man. These are the perennial mysteries of marriage and it's wiser for all those outside to step back and say, 'Whatever the truth, we have to move beyond recrimination.' Always I plead for forgiveness; it's the only thing that can break those cycles.

Now, all your attempts at communication have failed. Yet actions speak louder than words and so the only advice I can give you is radical. You won't like it but something has to give. Write to your sons telling them you will pull off your solicitor and relinquish your claim on the house for now, *if* they meet you for a talk. You tell me you're in 'financial difficulty' and yet you have the priceless gift of a loving partner and (presumably) a roof over your head. Do you *really* need to take their roof? Whatever 'stress and sadness' you experience is triplicated in what was once your family home. Some deal could be done where you leave well alone until such time as your boys leave home (soon, surely?) and your husband can move somewhere smaller. Such magnanimity may hurt your purse but it may heal all your hearts.

If we could read the secret history of our enemies,
we would find in each person's life sorrow and
suffering enough to disarm all hostility.

Henry W. Longfellow (American poet, 1807–82)

27

THE SAME SOUL

The letter was from a wife whose husband has dementia and is now
in a care home. Her adult son and daughter responded to her sadness
with a brisk 'But he's not dead.'

'D BE ASTONISHED to meet anyone who did not regard your
quiet, personal story of love and loss as serious and universal. The
news may be full of international economics, yet what happens to
our own loved ones will always seem more important than anything
else. This goes beyond self-centredness, since how we respond to
those around us is (I believe) an illustration of the butterfly theory.
Do you know what I mean? That a butterfly flapping its wings here
can cause a storm somewhere else. So the way we treat *this* person
here adds to (or detracts from) what George Eliot called 'the growing good of the world'.

That's why I'm sorry your son and daughter fell short. Had they shown more understanding, you would not be feeling quite so worried about your feelings. They should have comforted you, told you not to feel guilty, reassured you it was fine to feel full of grief. You need loving support, not to be made to feel like a freak, determined to bottle up those natural feelings of loss. To be charitable, maybe they are so wrapped up with their children, and so ignorant about dementia, they did not know any better. But my message to everybody reading this is – for heaven's sake, be more sensitive! Oh, and become better informed about Alzheimer's disease, because it affects all of us, directly or indirectly.

First, Linda, it sounds to me as you are already doing all the right things. Please realise that you're certainly not 'just a visitor' but a still-vital part of his life. Acting from the heart, you need to allow your heart its sadness – to know that you are allowed to feel as you do, tears and all. You have indeed 'lost' the husband who made you smile for all those years, and it must often feel as if you do not know this vulnerable Bill who inhabits the same body. He has changed in un-obvious ways, like suddenly being interested in watching birds and squirrels as he never was before. Can I suggest you try to see this not as evidence that his life is 'empty and joyless', but that it can still be renewed in unexpected ways? The small living creatures give him pleasure, so take in bird seed and those fatty treats that hang. I wonder if you might put up bird posters in his room, and get some CDs of birdsong, setting up a player so all he has to do is press the button? The Royal Society for the Protection of Birds has some lovely presents for him in its online shop, including various soft toys (no, they are not childish but provide comfort) in many bird shapes that 'sing' the appropriate songs.

I'd like to think you were in touch with others, too. The

Alzheimer's Society has two branches in your area and I think it would do you good to swap experiences in order to feel less alone. The internet would certainly help you; I suspect you don't use it (as you didn't email) and so this would be a useful thing for your children to teach you. Get a second-hand computer; it would put you in touch with a community of relatives like yourself – as well as being a resource for those grandchildren.

You still give Bill so much devoted care, but you mustn't become exhausted and depressed. If you bottle up your feelings you store up trouble for later, so please don't. Making sure you have new things in your own life (e.g. the computer) will help you find the energy to go on adding to his. When you sit quietly and hold his hand you give him comfort, and I hope it may comfort you a little to reflect that the soul of the man you love is still the same, although within an altered person. A reader sent me the beautiful 'Alzheimer's Prayer', which ends 'And finally, Lord, let them know how much their visits mean, how even through this relentless mystery I can still feel their love.' Please imagine your husband saying those words to you.

Two weeks later

AND FINALLY...

Recently I replied to a letter from 'Linda' whose husband was in a care home, suffering from Alzheimer's disease. Linda was permanently distressed, as well as guilty. She also did not know how to handle her husband's condition. Her letter moved many of you to write understanding letters, and (because I suggested she encourage her husband's new interest in the bird table) the RSPB kindly sent some gifts. Several readers recommended a book by Oliver James, *Contented Dementia*. I bought it and can confirm that anybody who wants help in caring for the condition will find this excellent work a revelation.

The good news is – Linda feels much better. She tells me:

I have begun to implement all you suggested for my husband and feel as if a huge, crushing weight has been lifted from me. I skip about, laugh, and everyone notices a change for the better. It was as if I needed permission from someone else – in this case, your good self – to do things for myself. Everything that benefits me benefits my husband. So I listen to music, go on long walks etc. Mainly I have accepted that I will feel this grief until Bill dies, but that I don't have to die with him. I thank you from the bottom of my heart, Bel, you're a saint...

Well, no! But if this page has a purpose beyond the individual problems it's the message that to be human is to be complicated and open to pain and that (in turn) the finest thing we can do is understand the pain of others. Linda's children dismissed her grief at the steady, daily 'loss' of the husband she loved so much. She needed a friend to say, 'Hey, it's all right. You're allowed to feel unhappy, but don't forget to look after yourself too.' Now I know problems can sometimes seem insurmountable, but please remember that words that simple can work. It's not a case of 'Pull yourself together and get on with it,' but, 'I'd feel just as bad in your shoes, so how can I help?'

28

SUFFER THE LITTLE CHILDREN

A READER, JANE, WROTE to me, in great distress, about the
case of Baby P (the seventeen-month-old English boy who
died in London in 2007 after suffering more than fifty injuries at the hands of his mother, her boyfriend and his brother over an
eight-month period, during which he was repeatedly seen by Harin-
gey Children's services and NHS health professionals). She begged
me to comment and asked, 'How can those monsters have inflicted
such torture on a beautiful, innocent little boy? I have a two-year-
old son and it has broken my heart.' Jane goes on, 'I'm not a religious
person, but how can any God let something like this happen?'

She begins her letter, 'This is not a personal problem.' Yet it is,
because it touches on universal grief as well as the horror that people
who wear a human face can do such evil that calls humanity into
question. We know they do, yet each time disbelief and outrage is
felt anew, as it should be. Similarly, the Archbishop of Canterbury
felt despair after 9/11 and many Jewish people have asked where
God was during the Holocaust. The very thought that – possibly

just a few streets away – the vilest aspects of humankind are being practised can invite darkness to spread over your own life.

It's like pollution. You feel irrationally guilty, as if somehow you should have been able to save *that* child – even if you accept it would be impossible to help the children of the Congo. And I find that one of the most disturbing aspects of cases like this is your *own* violent impulse towards the murderers. When I think of Baby P *I* want to kill. Thus they make you – even for a few seconds – as evil as they are. And yet ... and yet ... is it not natural to want vengeance? To thirst for punishment? As one who often counsels pardon, I have to acknowledge the limits of forgiveness.

But, the fact that Jane took up pen and paper to communicate her acute sorrow shows the very compassion that is our saving grace – the only hope we have of combating evil. Oh yes, we need vigilance too, and strong systems, and an eternally critical eye on the way we operate as a society, and so on. Yet we also have to acknowledge what Auden wrote: 'Those to whom evil is done do evil in return.' That bitter truth is at the heart of most cases of child abuse.

In the end, Jane, I have no answers – except to suggest translating compassion into action. It's too late to help one tragic baby, but the NSPCC is desperate for funds to help thousands; £100 pays for a month's treatment for a child traumatised by abuse, while ChildLine doesn't yet have the resources to deal with the astonishing volume of calls it gets. Children's charities – *all* of them – perpetually need funds and this is a vital way to help suffering children be heard.

29

A MEMORY OF HAPPINESS

This reader left her abusive, drunk partner, taking their son with her. Six
years on, she is doing well, but worries about the life she has given her
child. She sees how her mother puts up with her boozy, bullying father, and
fears a pattern: 'Sometimes I ask myself, when will life get better? Will it
always be so tough? Is this what it's all about? I think back to when I was
a child and my dad took me to the farm where he grew up and I think I will
never be that happy again. I wish my son could experience such happiness.
Is there any hope for me?'

A
T THE END your letter you offered us a snapshot – when
the shutter of your soul clicked and you felt happy. You
and your dad at the place he loved (else he wouldn't have
taken you there) and him sharing it just with you – when love was
uncomplicated and the space of the summer sky seemed endless.
Before you saw what your father could be like. Before you fell for a

man just like him. There will be such glittering moments in most lives, no matter how unlucky, beset by poverty, beaten by circumstance, heartbroken at the end of love or the end of a beloved life.

Just as we all go on easily reliving the painful moments (yes, I remember when I was nine and somebody pushed me down the ice-slide in the playground and everybody laughed) so do we have to teach ourselves to retrieve the good. I'm grateful to you for (accidentally) suggesting an exercise for us all, to help us through dark days. Let's all make ourselves revisit one time when we felt truly happy. 'Can't' isn't allowed in this game. Where were you? Who with? What did the place look like? Was there a scent in the air? Dig out such a recollection (no matter how trivial, like a new Dinky Toy) and play with it, like a ball tossed from hand to hand. It's yours.

You see, when the ball is in your hand you don't have to let it go. I want you to seize on your own memory of happiness as the measure of how things can be, and vow to trace a path back to the 'you' who was there. This is where the hope is. This is what you can give your son.

A poem by Mary Oliver asks this question: 'What will you do with your one, wild, precious life?' This is a fantastic challenge (which we could all print on a Post-it note to stick on the mirror) and 'don't know' isn't allowed either. In your case, you rose to the challenge when you chose to leave your abusive relationship so decisively. You have created a decent, independent life for you and your son out of that chaos and should praise yourself for that. Why do you say, 'I know I have not done all I can for my little boy?' None of us can ever do 'all' for our children because we are not super-people or saints; all we can do is our best. Stop blaming yourself.

You say you have 'sought counselling' more than once, so know the benefits. If you've developed claustrophobia and have attempted to find a cure, you're clearly aware of your own psychological state. But maybe you should ask whether this phobia could be triggered by a feeling of entrapment within your life. You see no way out – therefore, by definition, you feel trapped. It's a key part of that anxiety disorder.

Yet you are that lady who so bravely walked. You took control of your life then, and you can do so again. For a start, please stop worrying about things impossible to control, like whether or not your one parent or other may develop dementia. There is also nothing you can do to mend your parents' relationship. And there is no point in wondering if you will meet another man because none of us can know who will cross our path, and (with your experience) you are wise to be wary.

Yet you *can* build on what you have already achieved, for the sake of your son. You can love him, help him with his shyness, be strong for him – but, above all, 'your one, wild, precious life' can give him the gift of experiences to match that long-ago one you cherish. Can you remember where that farm was – and take him there? It might be a fruitful journey for both of you. And try asking your son what his own favourite memory is. You may find you have already given him happiness to last a lifetime.

Out of life comes death,
and out of death, life;
Out of the young, the old,
and out of the old, the young...

Heraclitus (Greek philosopher, 530–475 BC)

30

A FLAME OF REMEMBRANCE

THREE MORNINGS AGO I lit a candle in my hall. Though I am not of the Jewish faith, this was a Yahrzeit candle, traditionally lit on the anniversary of a death (actually, the night before, but I quail at the fire risk) to burn throughout the day. It was a symbol of my remembrance of the birth/death-day of my second son, Tom, who would have reached the age of thirty-three. Inevitably, I wonder what he'd have been like. A doctor? A dancer? A dad? All possibility lost. Yet the candle gave comfort: a reminder that Something Happened, never to be forgotten.

By chance, a friend came to see me, widowed nine months ago. Despite the depth of her sorrow she wants no counselling, believing she must make the dark journey herself. Her husband is always present in their house, she said, and that gives strange comfort. For how can something just end – something that was so wonderful? We agreed that it can't. And although she is not a religious person, she told me that the phrase 'gone before' now seems to have meaning. It is a light within the tunnel of her sadness…

The next day was the great American festival of Thanksgiving, when families gather to light candles and eat turkey in celebration of the Pilgrim Fathers' survival in a hostile land. It made me reflect how important it is to give thanks (especially in dark times) for what we have, but for what we have lost too. Give thanks for our beloved dead. My friend told me that she feels 'blessed' to have had all those years with her husband – and that (it seems to me) is part of her learning.

For love is, indeed, endless. There is no comparing the ache at the loss of a long, happy marriage with my own ache at the thought of the tiny baby I knew through nine months in the womb. Yet he too was part of my life's lessons, and I am grateful for that. My candle was indeed one of celebration – and in a sense, what my baby taught me is written here, each week.

Reason has moons; but moons not hers
Lie mirrored in her sea,
Confounding her astronomers,
But oh! – delighting me.

Ralph Hodgson (English poet, 1871–1962)

31

THE STAR ABOVE THE PATH

This story is almost too sad and complicated to summarise; you will get the gist from my reply. Violet's question is, 'What do you do when all your tricks don't work any more? ... Is there anything you can point me towards – or is this me now forever?'

A COUPLE OF weeks ago I bought myself an early Christmas present. Self-indulgent, I know, but the small woodcut beckoned – and I gave in. Art is my passion and the mood of the black-and-white image, made in 1922 by the artist Paul Nash, seemed to speak to me ... about this column. It shows a wooden fence, it's open gate leading into a dark wood. The trees are thick, impenetrable. There is no sky. And it takes a second before you notice that on the path leading into the depth of the wood is a frail female figure. Is she moving forward? Has she stopped? Impossible to tell.

All I know is that the little figure reminded me of all who write in with problems – and that although the dilemma might concern a broken marriage, unrequited love, children estranged, difficult parents or the agonising loneliness of an empty house, somehow they merge into the image of a person trying to find a way through a wood. No wonder one of Europe's greatest writers, Dante, opened his *Divine Comedy* (written in the fourteenth century) with the words, 'Midway upon the journey of our life, I found myself within a dark forest, for the straightforward pathway had been lost.'

So Josie writes, 'Where do I begin? My life is an unbelievable mess. There doesn't seem to be a single area that isn't in turmoil.' And here is Greg: 'I'm twenty-seven and my life is deeply unfulfilling. I'm out of step with everyone I meet and it's casting a long shadow over my life.' Anna pleads, 'I hope you can help me as I do feel very stuck in my life and that I have not moved on since the separation.' For 79-year-old Philip the issue is simple: 'How do you go on living when you can't see the way forward?'

I must be honest with you all and confess that I often feel lost within my own wood, unable to give a personal answer to every letter and overwhelmed by the sorrows of others.

The fragments I've quoted from others apply to you, don't they? It's as if I can pull back (as they do in movies) from the little picture propped on my desk, and see the bigger picture: other paths through the same wood, each carrying an individual soul on its journey. And the sad thing is, none of the people can glimpse each other. Nor can they see that above the trees, glittering in the bitter night sky, are countless stars, and among them one particular brilliant celestial light, showing the way. The Christmas reference will be immediately obvious. This is the time of year when, for many people, problems seem insurmountable – especially when the newspapers are full of depressing news, and money worries add to the emotional ones. Those who are lonely feel more isolated. Those who are divorced feel wistful for the ideal of married/family life. Those who are shy see bright satin dresses (at sale prices) in shop windows and feel sad or bitter that they have no parties to go to. Those who are old think back to happy Christmases of their youth and wonder where it all went – the lost time, the lost promise.

There is no magic formula – but I do believe that it might help us all to see the guiding star as a metaphor: something we can interpret and use for ourselves. Think of it as there all the time – even though it may be hidden by clouds or the canopy of trees. Visualise it with all your strength. It is the beginning of the journey – and none of us can know where it is leading. Only that the way is forward.

It's interesting that you think that writing something down counts – because a lot of people do indeed find the process therapeutic. Now you have written out (at far greater length than we have room for) something of your history and your current confusion and despair, I don't think you should stop. It would be good for you to make a careful list of all the gifts you find under your Christmas tree this year: that brilliant friend who understands you so well; the wonderful son who makes you so proud; the supervisor who cares for your welfare; the memory of the superb counsellor who changed you – and will again, if you conquer your fear. Then what of the courage that enabled you to leave a bad marriage; the fact that you could love again (no matter what the outcome, it is the *capacity* for love we celebrate); the sheer nobility that enabled you to take care of your ex's new child; your discovery of the joy of charity shop dressing before it became fashionable…?

I point you towards all those glittering truths.

Naturally I want you to go back to counselling as well as to make yourself socialise with your friend – and you know why? Because taking those steps forward will be good for your adored son, as well as for you. So I beg you to do what you already know you must. You're on the way, you know – stumbling forward on the path, like the rest of us. But please – just look up and see what's in the sky. And (another 'trick' to aid your courage) sing to yourself the Leonard Cohen lyric that – forgiving all – ends in rejoicing: *Hallelujah*.

I stood in the cold on the porch
And could not think of anything so perfect
As man's hope in the face of darkness.

Richard Eberhart (American poet, 1904–2005)

32

A MATTER OF PRINCIPLE

Dear Bel,

Is a Principle worth finishing a relationship for? This is important.

JOAN

T HIS IS THE shortest letter I have ever received, and although
sometimes I sigh at the pages and pages of painful detail I
receive from other readers, now I yearn for some from you. For
you do indeed raise an important point, but my instinctive answer
– without any knowledge of the story attached to your question –
can only be 'That depends.'

Think about that word 'story'. I live in a house stuffed with books.
There are stories on my shelves, from Greek and Roman myths,
through Beowulf, the greats of centuries of English literature, to

modern writers like Margaret Atwood and Philip Roth. I love the thrillers of James Lee Burke and Ruth Rendell. Then what about the life stories? There are biographies, memoirs, histories and books of psychotherapy containing fascinating case studies. I have two whole shelves of plays (oh, the menace of the late Harold Pinter…) and far more poetry books than I could possible begin to count – which build to a cumulative story of each poet's heart, mind, soul.

What do I learn from all these pages – the starting point to any answer to your question? That while there may be only so many plot outlines, reworked again and again, the human story is so various, so rich, so complicated that writers always find fresh ways of interpreting it. And always will. I'm imagining somebody asking Shakespeare your question. He goes away, ponders a while – then writes *King Lear* and *Othello* and *Measure for Measure*, to name but three. Then he set his mind to the great dilemmas of rulers … Philosophers may toil away at working out systems of principles, but writers are more likely to shrug and say, 'Surely it depends? Tell me the story…'

If a woman (or man) pronounces, 'In terms of fidelity I believe in the "one strike and you're out" principle,' I'll probably shake my head and reply, 'How do you know how you'll feel if it happens?' For what do you do if a spouse makes a terrible mistake and strays then asks for forgiveness? Kick them out on principle? Or take them back according to an equally valid principle of giving somebody you love a second chance? After all, people bomb and murder on matters of principle (look at the Middle East, just for a start), so I've never been convinced that abstract principles are a sensible code for life. Principles can so easily become rank prejudice. Monsters often justify their actions by invoking principle.

Of course we need rules – but ones worked out through an

understanding of humanity and operated with imagination. So this woman's husband is unfaithful and she takes him back. She then says, 'Of course, you realise that the consequences of broken trust will live with us. I can forgive, but it's impossible to forget. So we *both* have to try hard, rebuild, talk together and be very, very careful – because if it happens again that really will be the end.' She is being pragmatic, realistic, honest – call it what you will. But I would say that she has to stick to that position, and probably not give him a second chance.

Ah, but notice how that 'probably' slipped in under the radar before I could stop it? You see, you might say, 'I only buy organic food on principle,' but will you let yourself starve if such food is unavailable?

You might say, 'On principle I will not tolerate a person who lies to me' – never speaking to them again – but what do you do if that person is your son or daughter? You might say, 'I find porn utterly revolting on feminist principles,' but what do you do if the man you adore confesses a fascination for the stuff?

I suppose my simple answer to your short question has to be, 'Not really.' To me the greatest principle we can live by is that of making kindness inform every action – which is another version of the great 'Do as you would be done by.' But in order to live by that principle you usually have to cut people some slack. If you wave a big stick of strict Principle at somebody you care for, you may well find that it hurts you too.

We can ask and ask but we can't have again what seemed ours forever – the way things looked ... a remembered voice, the touch of a hand, a loved face. They've gone and you can only wait for the pain to pass.

J. L. Carr, *A Month in the Country* (1980)

33

LOVE AND VALOUR

ACH YEAR I hang a heart-shaped garland (made red from berries and beads) for a few days on my front door, to mark the feast of St Valentine. Stories about the origins of Valentine's Day are fascinating and the billion cards sent worldwide prove that at this time of year people need the lovers' festival. But I wouldn't be doing my job if I didn't point out that the hardest part of a relationship begins when the first flush of romance is over. And what about in a long marriage? How can people keep the imaginary heart on their front door?

St Valentine's name derives from the Latin word '*valens*', meaning 'Strong' or 'worthwhile'. We'd all want our relationships to fit that definition, wouldn't we? Soppy romantic love is all very well, but it can't last without a more serious underpinning; think 'valour' and 'valiant' too – which love requires.

Taking each letter of the Latin word as a starting point, here's my Valentine advice for established couples who feel they are … well … just rubbing along:

Value each other for what you first loved when you met, and honour it each day – for although people change, the core person you remember is still there, waiting to be rediscovered.

Admit your own failings as readily as you point out your partner's, so that they may even cancel each out – and always avoid the accusatory 'You…'

Laugh together as much as possible (especially at yourselves) because it helps you to *like* each other and that's one way of feeding long-lasting love.

Empathise with your partner, because putting yourself in somebody else's shoes can help you understand why they are driving you mad – or how sad they are.

Notice your partner's daily needs and take care of them, which means anything from a much-needed hug to the offer of tea and sympathy.

Share as much as you can, for even if you have different interests you can still ask questions, while doing things together gives you something to talk about – which feeds the heart.

34

THE CHINK IN THE WALL

This 43-year-old lady's husband had an affair (with the young au pair) but
she forgave him and rebuilt the marriage. Eight years ago, he restarted that
relationship and now she is in the middle of a painful divorce: 'The point is how
will I ever trust again? We were married for sixteen years – and now I have a brick
wall in front of me and do not know how to knock it down. How do I move on?'

Y OU ARE ASKING a key question: how do I cope with loss?
At the end of a marriage we do feel bereaved and the sense
of loss drives you back in time, right to the beginning, when
you met. Everything is called into question, even the happiest times.
At this stage I think I should answer your simple question about
moving on with a simple answer. Since divorce is so traumatic, do
not expect to 'move on'. Not yet. Thinking that you *should* places
another burden on you – which you don't need. Knocking down a
wall requires far too much sweat.

Instead of glib prescriptions for 'moving on' – I want you to contemplate that brick wall. Solid, eh? But you know, the laws of quantum physics tell us that nothing is solid – everything is constantly moving and changing. Strangely, in the same way, the laws of poetry ask us to see beauty and possibility in all things – yes, even the worst. Even a brick wall.

I'd like you to read these two lines from a poem/song by Leonard Cohen a couple of times before we go on:

> *There is a crack, a crack in everything.*
> *That's how the light gets in.*

If you think of a crack in a structure, it's a sign of weakness. A cracked wall will be susceptible to frost. A cracked Ming vase has lost value. Many marriages have a fatal flaw, a crack that isn't visible at the beginning, but which means the couple will not survive. The roots will probably be in the childhood of one or other (or both) partner and the motives often go beyond the purely sexual...

But what about Cohen's 'crack' that lets in the light? If you were in a pitch-black room, the tiniest chink in the outer wall would admit a fine ray of light to relieve the darkness. You probably wouldn't have noticed the chink until the terrible, total gloom made it visible. Cohen is suggesting that this is indeed a way to view misfortune. Nothing is perfect – we have to accept that. It goes with being human and mortal. Yet it is through coping with imperfection that we learn and grow. It is how we respond to our pain that makes all the difference. I'd like you to see that truth as what your brick wall is telling you.

That the man you fell in love with, married, and blessed once with your forgiveness should so deceive you is good grounds for anger, disillusion and mistrust.

But it is how you process those feelings that will make all the difference. At the moment, your self-esteem is very low. It's not just that you think you will never trust another man again, it is that you doubt any man would love you – the rejected and deceived one. From my perspective, you were brave and mature when you decided (that first time) that 'the whole picture' of the marriage was more important than a principle. This was wise, not (as some might think) foolish. But when he cheated again you were equally brave, mature and wise to call time. So I would like you to start seeing yourself as strong, rather than a victim. That will help you remove just one brick from that wall, and let through a whole beam of sunlight.

Your strength (for now) consists in holding things together for those children and devoting yourself to them. Think about how well you have done this, and (in realising what that says about you) remove another brick. Now you can peep though – and see the view. Believe me when I tell you that the path you see stretching ahead belongs to you – and you cannot possibly know where it will lead or who you will meet along the way. Soon you will step forward and find that the wall melts away – having done its job. Perhaps, you see, it was protecting you from too many choices before you were ready to take them. 'Moving on' happens when you realise that the person you need to trust is yourself.

A few weeks later

AND FINALLY...

Two weeks ago I printed a letter from 'Deborah' who was going through a bitter divorce after her husband's repeated infidelity and felt up against 'a brick wall'. Her situation struck a chord with many of you; I was moved by the sympathetic tone of your letters. For example, Nigel 'read the article with tears in my eyes' because he has been through the same situation, and wants Deborah to know that she 'does have a future'. Colin's ex-wife was also unfaithful and he writes, 'My point to Deborah is that, yes, time does heal (as it has for me) but you have to focus firmly on the future ... I would like Deborah to know that she will be able to bounce back and regain that missing trust.'

Susie saw incredible parallels with her own story, and says that getting her divorce 'lifted the darkness unbelievably'. She goes on: 'I haven't met anyone else, nor am I looking, but I feel it will happen and I would be receptive. It's human nature to trust and to see the good in people – that was the thing I was determined to hang on to.'

Twelve years after the horror of her own divorce, Petra wants us to know how good life can be. She shed much weight, went on dates and single holidays, started a counselling course and at sixty-five has just got a new job. She says, 'I've grown to understand that life throws all it can at you but you will survive and learn from all the experiences. I have the love of my children and grandchildren and wish I could give Deborah a hug and say it will be OK.' There were many others in the same vein – and Penny recommends the Divorce Recovery Workshop because it helped her so much, as did a book called *Growing Through Divorce* by Jim Smoke.

As for Deborah herself, she wrote, 'I cannot tell you how perfect the advice was and how it fitted into my life!' and says she does believe me when I assure her that the brick wall will melt away in time.

Not everything that is faced can be changed, but nothing can be changed until it is faced.

James Baldwin (American novelist and playwright, 1924–87)

We often freeze in the face of difficulties, lacking the will or drive to move forward – but those very difficulties are time for blind faith in our own capabilities, to pluck up courage, make the leap...

Lorenzo Quinn (Italian sculptor, b. 1966)

35

MY FATHER'S FUNERAL

Dear Bel,

My childhood was hideously dysfunctional and I've been estranged from my father for eighteen years. Two weeks ago, my brother (who's been in contact with him for the last five years) called me to say he was dying and he wanted to see me. I went to see him. It was a heartbreaking visit, he looked so old; I told him I was sorry the way our lives turned out and I cried a lot. I met his new family for the first time at the hospital, which was all very strange. He died three days after that, aged eighty-seven.

I felt at peace when I heard he'd died – then suddenly last week I got seriously mad at the whole situation. I've spent years trying to forget about my dad, and now all that pain is back again. He's being buried next week and that's my problem. Do I go to the funeral or not? Something in me doesn't want to go. I feel I don't belong there, I feel almost hypocritical about going to pay my last 'respects' to a man who I know didn't want me and who treated us all so badly. I initially thought that I'd go and support my brother, stand with him, but I'm not sure now. It just doesn't feel right – any of it. I feel torn – I don't know if I want to go, or if I am expected to go? Please tell me what you think.

Maryline.

YOU ARE RIGHT that nothing feels right, because your life to date has been a long, painful attempt to deal with all the problems of that childhood – about which you told me in far more detail than there's room for here. Understanding all that, I have to tell you I'm in no doubt whatsoever that you should go to the funeral. No doubt it will be difficult and upsetting (as all funerals are) but if you don't go you will be storing up these horrible, negative, angry feelings, and if you do go, maybe some of them will come out and be buried (or burnt up) with him.

I repeat, I have no doubt.

Your father didn't want you when you needed him but he did seek to put things right at the end. He asked for you – and surely there has to be the possibility of forgiveness, for all of us. That is what he wanted – and in a sense your tears began the process of washing you all clean. You can never forget the harm he did, but I do believe you can acknowledge the fact that his genes are a part of you, and bow your head to say goodbye at the end. You are not paying 'respects', you are acknowledging what was, and what is no more.

Your place is, indeed, at your brother's side. You say you don't know if you 'want' to go or if you are 'expected' to go. Of course you do not *want* to go and it doesn't matter one cent if anybody *expects* you to go. All that matters is that it is the proper thing – for your own inner peace of mind, for closure – to go. If it helps your brother than that's a great plus too. Be brave, girl. It's the only way to be.

...every deep feeling is like a peach, to be eaten straight from the tree of life, not spoiled by pawing and pressing.

Seán Ó Faoláin (Irish writer, 1900–91)

Seek out the good in every man,
And speak of all the best you can.

Geoffrey Chaucer (English poet, 1343–1400)

36

A SAMPLE OF SYMPATHY

EASTER BROUGHT ME an entirely unexpected gift – and I'm so pleased! A choc-lover, I got plenty of that food of the gods, but my husband also pushed the boat out to give me a special something I really wanted. I've always loved samplers – the embroidered pictures young girls sewed in the nineteenth century, 'sampling' all their meticulous embroidery stitches and usually adding religious messages, their name and the date. You see them in museums and I've always loved to imagine the little girls patiently sewing – and wondering what sort of lives they had.

I hinted to my husband (don't we all do that?) that one day we must buy a sampler for our home. He's a prudent sort of chap, so imagine how amazed I was when he handed me the parcel. The sampler he chose has two tiny embroidered lambs (which look like our funny little lapdog) as well as the usual flowers and birds. But best of all is the uplifting rhyme – which happens to be perfect for an advice columnist. It would be a good motto for an Agony Aunts' Trade Union!

This is the little prayer thirteen-year-old Sarah Marchant embroidered, around 1825 (unusually, it's undated, but the experts can tell by the linen):

> *Teach me to feel another's woe,*
> *To hide the faults I see,*
> *The Mercy I to others show*
> *That Mercy show to me.*

It's good advice for all of us – to feel the pain of others, not to pick on obvious faults in them, and to show the kind of understanding, sympathy and forgiveness (all wrapped up in the one word 'mercy') to other people that you want for yourself. Yes, I know it's hard. But throughout history it's been worth a try.

37

SECRET GUILT

Melanie had a two-week fling with a colleague, makes no excuses and is racked by guilt. To make things worse, she is now pregnant by her husband and believes she will be punished for her sin: 'I pray every day for forgiveness and am truly, truly sorry for what I did. I know I don't deserve to be happy but I don't know what to do. This is the first (and maybe the last) time I have told anyone my secret; I can't even tell my oldest closest friends, or my GP, as I am so ashamed of what I did. I need your advice.'

I T'S STRANGE YOUR letter should come just as I finished *The Secret Scripture*, by the Irish writer Sebastian Barry. Relevant to you is what the main character, old Roseanne McNulty, tells her secret journal about a terrible mistake she made when she was young, at a turbulent time in Ireland's politics when the priesthood and the gun ruled the land.

Beautiful Roseanne is married to Tom, whom she loves. But she encounters strange John Lavalle whom she first met as a teenager. He tells her she is beautiful, that he will be at a certain place up on the mountain at 3 p.m. on Sundays. Driven by something she doesn't understand, Roseanne goes to meet him. She says, 'I knew what it was and how it looked but I didn't know what drove me up that mountain.' That impulse destroys her life. Although nothing happens between the couple, they are spotted by a priest – and that's enough to render Roseanne immoral and beyond the pale. Her punishment is truly terrible and lasts a lifetime.

Do we still believe in sin and punishment, in the same way? No – but this is one of those times when I wish you could enter a Catholic confessional and whisper through the grille to someone you believe can absolve you. I'd wish you that comfort, Melanie, because I am moved by the anguish in a letter written by a good woman who made one bad mistake and is profoundly sorry, but deserves happiness as much as any one of us. Your letter is full of dignity; you refuse to make excuses for yourself but admit to 'the thrill of another man finding me attractive'. Ah yes – let she who is without sin cast the first stone. I can't…

If you literally 'pray every day for forgiveness' then any Christian will tell you that you already have it. Your genuine remorse is the key. So take some deep breaths (I always advise this, since we need to stop and calm ourselves and deep breathing is the start) and focus on your unborn baby. From this moment on you have to realise (a) that nothing bad will happen because of what you did, and (b) this child is an innocent who needs to you to take of him or her with every single part of you. That means resting, eating, breathing and *willing* everything to be all right. Oh, and praying too, if you like – for the three of you.

The issue of confession is difficult when it comes to your husband. What can I tell you but my instinctive response – which is to keep silent? I know some readers will angrily accuse me of counselling deception. So be it. What he does not know cannot hurt him – unless, that is, you continue in this state of panic. Stop. The risk associated with telling him is, in my considered opinion, too great. You love him and you love his unborn child and that love will only grow in power when you are a family – and far outweigh the mistake you made and quickly rectified.

Of course, you will always carry the guilt with you in a private part of your mind, but many people live with guilty secrets. It's a part of the human condition, making you no worse than many others. Believe me, it is *not* an 'easy option' to remain silent, for sometimes people blurt and inflict far more damage than if they'd been stronger and held their tongues. Sometimes they confess in order to punish the other person, not to wipe their souls clean. The human spirit is very complex – and that thought takes me back to your unborn child. You *must* forget yourself now, park this fruitless angst in its secret place, and concentrate on the precious little person who is capable of bringing great joy to you and your husband. Let me end with the words that begin Sebastian Barry's fine book: 'The world begins anew with every birth.'

If you will tell me why the fen
Appears impassable, I then
Will tell you why I think that I
Can get across it if I try.

Marianne Moore (American poet, 1887–1972)

38

MERSEY MANIA

GLADLY WE HEADED north for the opening of an exhibition called 'The Mersey Sound' at the Victoria Gallery at Liverpool University. For me it was a nostalgic double-whammy, because I was born and brought up in Liverpool, so driving into that glorious city and breathing in that fresh wind off the Mersey always does me good. Then came the poetry. Some of you will remember that when Penguin published the work of Adrian Henri, Roger McGough and Brian Patten in 1967, it was like a window being thrown open. I'll never forget it. Henri told us that 'Love is fish and chips on winter nights', McGough wrote of a girl's 'shoes with broken high ideals' and Patten wrote a song, 'Somewhere between Heaven and Woolworths'.

This was the poetry of real life, smoky parties, Batman and Beatlemania – and my generation lapped it up.

But not just my generation. *The Mersey Sound* is one of the biggest-selling anthologies of all times, always being reprinted. Now I'm wondering if young people will go to the Victoria Gallery and ask their parents, 'Was it really that wild?' Great material is displayed: original typed poems (much more eloquent than computer prints), wacky '60s posters, paintings by the great Henri (who became a friend of mine and died in 2000), and of course the black-and-white snaps of another age. All they need is 'The Scaffold' playing on a loop.

Anyway, Patten and McGough read magnificently and later there was (for the hard core of us) a merry quaffing of wine and noisy talk until well after midnight. The message of the evening was that poetry, like music, goes on talking to people of all ages, forever. Just think, the year *The Mersey Sound* was published, the Beatles released the *Sgt Pepper* LP – on which a famous track asked, 'When I get older losing my hair / Many years from now / Will you still be sending me a Valentine / Birthday greetings bottle of wine?'

YES, is the answer! Time has caught up with us all but we can always love the sense that in our hearts we are (to switch to Paul Simon) 'still crazy after all these years'.

39

LONELY SELF-PITY

Meet lonely Adrian (fifty) who works and then hangs about because there's nothing else in his life: 'It's a horrible downward spiral, and the longer you're alone, the harder it seems to be to find something to talk about. People at work gave up long ago asking if I had a nice weekend. My answer is always the same – No!'

WHEN I FIRST read your letter I was overwhelmed with a feeling of compassion for this lonely man with nothing in his life except work. But forgive me – on second and third readings I began to feel as frustrated by you as you are by your lonely, empty life. I can't do this job unless I'm honest – and there is a part of me that would like to take you by the shoulders and shake you out of this terrible, tedious self-pity.

You are absolutely right to guess that many letters arrive from people afflicted by terrible loneliness. It seems to be a modern disease, all the more shocking in the age of mass communication. Here's three in one postbag:

1. L (forty-seven) 'woke up two weeks ago and realised the opportunity to have the life I wanted has passed me by'. She has been taking care of an elderly parent, had 'no job and consequently no colleagues' and 'I don't know how to make friends with either men or women.'

2. Katie (seventeen) doing A levels: 'I feel like in the future I am going to have no friends and be very lonely. I wish I could change my personality...'

3. Sarah (thirty-five) has 'no home of my own and no husband and children and I feel that it is too late and my life is all downhill...'

I would guess that L and Sarah are suffering from depression and should get help, whereas Katie is enduring her parents' divorce so has every reason to be straightforwardly unhappy. But I'd like you to think about them for a few seconds – and feel too, for a reader who is dying of cancer and wants to live, live, live. There are so many people out there, Adrian, and then there's you, locked in your prison. It is obvious that you need help. Need to go out there and do the obvious thing: pay for proper counselling (you have a salary) to help kick-start your life. Have you not thought of this? If you do read this column every week you will know how often I tell people that they have to be pro-active and seek help.

If you 'live on chocolate, crisps and vodka' you probably have unhealthy-looking skin, hair and teeth, not to mention a spreading middle. Not attractive – and certain to increase depression. If you answer your work colleagues with endless negatives, they won't want to ask you anything … If your response to loneliness is to 'mooch' about supermarket cafés and bars rather than join any one of hundreds of classes or voluntary activities that would force you to interact with people – then you have the imagination of a flea. Do you know how you 'find a friend'? Not by 'wishing', but by taking an interest in other people: asking questions, reaching out, realising that behind the most confident-seeming person are individual worries, hope and fears, waiting to be shared. If only someone will ask.

You ask why I don't pass on emails. Because I cannot take on that responsibility (even if there were time) since the risk could be that a stalker (say) made contact through me. But suggesting I do that is surely scarcely different from contacting a lonely-hearts site, which you say you don't have the confidence to do! It doesn't take much to start online chats with women and who knows where it might lead? Try it.

Here comes a phrase I swore I would never use: *Pull yourself together*. Believe me, Adrian, I do understand about the 'downward spiral', but you *can* stop this endless plunge. Vow to do one new, positive thing each day (as above) and I promise you that spring will brighten for you, as surely as the leaves will burst from the bare branches all around.

One month later

AND FINALLY…

K nowing you like catch-ups, I bring good news about Adrian. Four weeks ago, I printed his lonely letter: he hated his life, lived on 'chocolate, crisps and vodka' and was full of misery and self-pity.

Unusually brisk, I told him to get his act together. A number of readers reproached me; one lady even said that if he committed suicide it would be my fault, which wasn't very nice.

But you see, sometimes a deep instinct tells me that sighing, 'Oh, you poor thing' isn't good enough. We all have to take control of our lives and if somebody goes to the trouble of writing such a long letter it's unlikely (though not impossible, I admit) they are suffering from clinical depression. Anyway, Adrian was grateful and found my advice 'a much-needed shot in the arm of reality' – and the first thing he did was start to repaint his flat. There's positive action!

It gets better. I nagged him privately by email after his letter was published, because I truly felt he would benefit from counselling and knew he was reluctant to try. So finally he went to the library to look up local counselling services – an excellent move, because at a computer you have no human interaction. For there at the library he got talking to a lady and now they are in a relationship. 'I count my blessings that we met,' says Adrian. He goes on: 'I'm eating proper food again. Before I wrote to you my kitchen cupboard contained one tin of baked beans and the entire stock of the off-licence. Now I have cut my alcohol intake to a fraction of what it was.' He cooks with his new lady and is trying to give up smoking because she doesn't like it. Adrian wants people to know that 'things CAN change and sometimes do so very quickly'. To my delight he says, 'Writing to you was a big step and a positive one and helped me get things moving.'

Now I am off to my jukebox to deafen myself with Hot Chocolate singing, 'I believe in miracles…'

40

GRIEF FOR A WIFE

Dear Bel,

My wife died five years ago and I am still grieving. My sons and daughter want to know – when will I find somebody else? I told them it is too early for me – my love is still with their mum. I am fifty-eight but not in good health. I know they have my best interests at heart, so what can I say to them? I don't want to hurt their feelings. And how long does grieving take? I do still love my wife. If or when I meet somebody else, will I be able to love her? And, you know, if the lady wanted the relationship to go further I am not sure about the physical side of things – whether I could. What will my wife want me to do?

Alan.

As you can imagine, I receive many sad letters from bereaved people, and most of them have at their heart the question 'How long?' But that question is, of course, impossible to answer. The bereavement experts have identified stages of grief and this kind of analysis can be useful – helping people to see that they aren't odd to feel as they do. On the other hand, human beings are not machines and there are no rules which say that after one year you should feel like *this* but after four years you should feel like *that*. Loss is at the centre of human existence: we learn it when we lose a beloved pet as a child (perhaps), or are rejected by the first love, or get divorced or are forced unwillingly to take early retirement … These are all losses – experienced differently by each individual – which rehearse us for the greatest loss: the death of a loved one. This is what you have gone through – and nobody (no matter how well-meaning) has the right to tell you it's time you moved on.

Perhaps you will never love another woman, Alan. But I'm sure your family would be happy if you found female companionship: someone to go for a walk with, or share a cream tea or a film. It doesn't have to involve sex, so I suggest you stop worrying about that now. If you were to meet a nice person through any activities you may be involved with (and that's *always* a good idea) then just take it slowly on a basis of friendship. Friendship is another form of love, after all. And the amazing thing about human beings is that love isn't like a cake that can be used up. Love is like a muscle that, if exercised, can grow stronger and be used in different ways.

So put on a cheerful face to your family and say, 'I'm working on it.' Go out, get busy and meet as many people as you want to. Try new things and remember that even if you feel low or unwell, just going into the flower shop and chatting to the florist while you treat yourself to a bunch of daffs will do you good. That is what your wife wants, isn't it? Good things for you? I like the fact that you speak of her in the present tense, because that reminds us of an important truth. We never truly 'lose' those we love, because we carry them with us, even if we can no longer see them. I'm sure you talk to your wife every day but I hope you also listen to her saying, 'Take care of yourself, love, and try to be happy.'

Words are so much the currency of our consciousness that we rely on them when they cannot take the weight. People who talk at grief, instead of holding hands with grief, are a menace. Words come later, but only after tears.

John Bowker (English theologian, b. 1935)

*I think the most necessary quality for anybody to have is
imagination. It makes people able to put themselves in other
people's places. It makes them kind and sympathetic.
It ought to be cultivated in children.*

Jean Webster (1876–1916), *Daddy-Long-Legs* (1912)

41

AN ELEVEN-YEAR-OLD
CALLS 'HELP'

Dear Bel,

I am eleven and ALWAYS read your pages in the *Mail*. I never thought it would be me writing in, but I'm faced with a problem, and need your help. We have a small family: my dad, mum, granddad and myself. The thing is, my dad lost his job last September but got a new one before Christmas, to start afterwards. Things were fine for about three months. Mum even admitted she had started enjoying herself more and felt complete again, knowing we were all happy. However, he lost his job again at the beginning of May and Mum went to pieces. Since then it has been row and row after row, and I just can't take any more. My parents are both hard-working people and I love them to pieces. Mum has been my rock all through life but now it seems I'm having to defend myself, as she seems weak in the mind. She does not have much faith in my dad any more and with the credit crunch things are getting harder. I'm also at private school, which means my parents have fees to pay and I'm SO worried and incredibly scared they'll get a divorce. We're in the middle of moving house too, so I keep trying to tell my mum she needs to focus on the new place instead of worrying. I'm in pieces and I know my mum feels broken in two. But I do not know how to make things better. PLEASE HELP. It would just give me some reassurance.

Summer.

WHEN YOU WERE little did you read fairy stories? I'm thinking of how many of them deal with problems the hero or heroine has to solve, like how to find your way out of the darkest, scariest wood. You know, you might just be the strongest one in your little family and it might help you a little to think of yourself as the heroine who *will* survive. Still, that's no consolation when you really long for family life to be peaceful. Believe me, even when you are a grown woman, the little girl inside you will still want to be looked after.

Your parents are enduring the worst of times. Moving house is itself one of life's most stressful experiences, even without the worry of your dad's unemployment. I expect the decision to move happened during that good time, and I wouldn't be surprised if they are regretting it – and blaming each other. The first thing you must tell yourself is that none of this is your fault. (In fact there is a very good website for young people you should look at: www.itsnotyourfault.org. Check it out to feel less alone.) I bet you worry that you being at private school makes things worse – and feel guilty. If so, you could tell your dad you wouldn't mind moving to the local state school (even if that's not true) if it would help the finances. That might make you feel 'in charge'. If you Google Relate+(your area) you'll discover the local office of the relationships charity, which helps young people too. You can talk to somebody on the phone, you know. And it might be helpful to keep a diary. If you write down your feelings – and vow to note down one thing that made you happy each day too – you'll find your journal becomes a real friend.

Do you get on with Granddad? It sounds as if you and he should make a sort of alliance, banding together to help Mum and Dad. But if he's not that sort of granddad, maybe your mum has a close friend you could talk to? It sounds like she is depressed and really should see someone. That would obviously benefit them both – but it's a hard thing for you to suggest because maybe they're too proud to seek help. That's why I wish you'd get a caring adult on your side. In the meantime, sit down with them one night and ask about when they met. Get them to remember funny stories; look at old snaps and laugh at their clothes; tell you how they felt when they knew you were coming along. Perhaps your secret quest is to help them remember they're a team who can face down troubles side by side. I feel so sorry for them, and for you, and understand how you feel more than I can tell you. But always remember they love you, even when they're so miserable they forget to show it.

The good news is that you are alive,
and the linden tree is still there,
standing firm in the harsh winter...
Leave behind the world of sorrows and preoccupation
and get free.

Thích Nhất Hạnh (Vietnamese Buddhist monk, b. 1926)

42

A SOULMATE?

Dear Bel,

How do you move on from the only person you ever loved? We're both in
our mid-fifties and had been with each other for almost eight years. I truly
loved him – he was so thoughtful and loving and always looked after me.
When we got together we'd had a rough time from our ex-partners ... but his
ex was more controlling even though they had been divorced for thirteen
years and she'd remarried. My two children stuck by us. His children were
adults with their own homes yet I was not allowed to visit them in case their
mother found out. In contrast, he was totally involved in most of our family
functions. When he had grandchildren I could visit only if the 'coast was
clear' – otherwise I was updated with photographs. During our time together
he retired but I didn't go to the 'do'. I knew something was wrong and later
found out he took his daughter's partner's mum back to his place until 6 a.m.
We split up but really missed each other and got back. Then his daughter got
married abroad and he didn't take me and – yes – the mum-in-law was there. I
can't tell you how hurt I was. We even got through that somehow.

He was always asking me to marry him but I was too scared to commit –
something always held me back. The crunch came when he started a new
job and over a weekend was bombarded with phone calls and texts from
a female work colleague. I finished it. Two years on I'm still hurting. I never
really believed in the 'soulmate' term before but I can tell you truly that he
was mine. I don't doubt that he loved me; I just mustn't have been quite
enough to keep him truly fulfilled. I'm not depressed and have a good social
network but there is a massive void in my life. I am missing my love.

Bridgit.

T
O BE HONEST, compared with some of the problems in my
postbag, yours didn't seem pressing. After all, at the end you
describe a situation many people worse off would find envi-
able … Looking again, it occurred to me that the issue at the heart
of your letter is also at the root of very many others – whether from
people who have been dumped, or married women with unfaithful
husbands, or sufferers from depression who wonder how to go on, or
bereaved souls bowed down by grief. The crux is a question people
have asked for centuries: how do we cope with loss? And it is loss –
the terrible ongoing sense of Absence – that afflicts so many of the
people who write to me.

Surely hope is essential to human survival; you describe this
ongoing feeling of deep disappointment that calls everything into
question. 'Life wasn't meant to be like this,' is the thought, facing
one's own sad reflection in the glass. Yet how do we know? Much is
talked and written about happiness, these days, even to the extent of

happiness lessons in some schools – and yet it seems to me that it's vital to face the fact that life is not a fairy tale and 'happy-ever-after' is a fantasy. I don't mean to be depressing. It's just that from my perspective people tend to be short on realism as well as self-knowledge. And that is a more serious 'void' than the longing for what cannot be.

In answer to your opening question, I'm going to be tough. You can 'move on' only by confronting the truth with more honesty than you've displayed. First, you say this man was the only 'person' you have ever loved, but that can't be true. You must have loved your first husband once, not to mention your children. You call the man you miss so much your 'soulmate' yet you persistently refused to marry him – which implies that he was not quite enough to keep *you* 'truly fulfilled'. You say 'he always looked after me' and yet he caved into his bullying ex and refused to stand up for you with regard to visiting his children and grandchildren. He didn't even take you to his retirement party – then behaved inappropriately with his son-in-law's mother! He didn't care that he hurt you and made you jealous. It so happens that I do *not* believe in the 'soulmate' illusion – but even if I did, I wouldn't describe a man who behaved like that as a perfect partner. Maybe what held you back from commitment to him was the knowledge that he was deeply flawed – but now you're looking back through rosy spectacles. It's time to take them off, accept that you and he shared bad times as well as good, and use what happened to learn something about yourself.

There is nothing any of us can do about the changes that happen to us – except to strive to make them happen *for* us. Like so many others, you've experienced great love and great sorrow. The challenge for you now is to learn to rejoice in the brave new life you are constructing – knowing that without the awareness of universal sadness we would have no means to transform that burden into grace.

Out beyond ideas of right-doing and wrong-doing, there is a field.
I'll meet you there.

Rumi (Persian poet and mystic, 1207–73)

43

A SISTER'S SUICIDE

This heart-breaking letter came from a sixty-year-old woman whose 'little sister' 'Hattie' took her own life three years earlier. Her teenage daughters found her 'hanging from a beam'. Now Hattie's widower has remarried, and 'the family seems happy' – but 'Edith' is single, misses her sister terribly and doesn't know how to cope, or 'move on'.

IRST LET ME say, quite simply, how sorry I am for you, for Hattie, for her family. This truly terrible action will always reverberate … and I suspect it will be impossible for you to 'move on' until you have analysed what you really feel about your sister's decision to take her own life, knowing she was bound to be discovered by her own daughters. Your journey of discovery may temporarily increase your pain, but I believe it necessary.

The eighteenth-century philosopher David Hume defended suicide by saying, 'A man who retires from life does no harm to society.'

But that's not true, is it? A man or woman who chooses suicide will blast apart the lives of his/her family and friends with all the destructive force of a bomb. In 1985, my novel *The Anderson Question* examined the effect of the apparently inexplicable suicide of a loved and respected village doctor on those around him. I created a wife full of shame and rage, who spat out, 'He did what he liked to himself, but that's not what I'm talking about. It's *me*. I can't forgive him for what he's done to *me*.'

I wonder if, deep in your soul, you have thought that too? You are allowed to feel anger and disbelief as well as grief. For Hattie 'chose' (I realise that the word is inaccurate) to smash a black hole into the life of each person who cared for her, and leave a legacy of guilt – expressed in your question: 'Why didn't I know how she was feeling and why couldn't I help?' You must have thought, sometimes bitterly, that your sister implicitly turned her back on your love. Doing so, she called into question all the care you gave her in childhood and seemed to turn the closeness you describe into a lie. I'm sure you've gone over telephone conversations, and conjured up how she looked the last time you saw her, searching for clues. She forced you to query whether you knew her at all – and that leads inevitably to the bewildering possibility that none of us can ever truly know another, and therefore our loves seem to fall into a terrifying black hole.

But they do not. We carry the love with us, no matter what happens. It's vital (having admitted some of the above) that you acknowledge all the wonderful things you and Hattie shared and don't let the end sully what was. Reaching the third anniversary will be painful. Light a candle for her and tell her aloud – yes, talk to that unquiet soul – that you remember this and that about her and that the best will remain with you forever. What you can do for her now is to look up one ordinary morning and notice something she would have liked, think of her during a piece of music, invoke her spirit as you tuck into a meal she loved – and in those moments know that all of us, in a sense, have a duty to experience our lives intensely, for the sake of the beloved dead who can no longer. Also, for her sake, you should play as large a part as possible in the lives of her girls.

But you have to acknowledge that you'll never know exactly why she did it. It could just as well have been something entirely inward and private, nothing to do with her doubts about where she lived or possible problems within her marriage. Speculation is fruitless. Look up Brian Patten's wonderful poem about loss called 'So Many Different Lengths of Time', which reflects on grief and asks how long it – like a human life – will last.

He writes:

> And the days will pass with baffled faces,
> then the weeks, then the months,
> then there will be a day when no question is asked,
> and the knots of grief will loosen in the stomach
> and the puffed faces will calm.

This is perhaps how you come to terms – by accepting that there are no terms.

*More helpful than all wisdom is one draught of
simple human pity that will not forsake us.*

George Eliot (1819–80), *The Mill on the Floss* (1860)

44

REMEMBER THE GOOD

ARE YOU A glass-half-full person? Personally, I still hold out my hopeful goblet each day, expecting it to be half-full of something delicious. The bad times – when I peer in miserably and wonder if it's actually half-empty and whether I have been deluded all these years – are few. Thank goodness.

And now I have Lloyd Gardner to thank for giving us all a reason to open something fizzy and fill our glasses to the very brim. I read about him a week ago and haven't been able to get that amazing 22-year-old out of my mind. Lloyd is the restaurant manager from Devon who was public-spirited enough to step forward and put the police on the trail of the dangerous, violent, loathsome man who brutally raped a woman and left her for dead. In a world where so many people are apathetic, that in itself was heartening.

Yet this young man then chose to give his £10,000 reward to the victim of the crime, who has been told that she will never fully recover from her injuries. Let me remind you of his words, because they chime with me like the most sublime poetry. 'I didn't feel like I'd earned it. The fact that such a horrific thing happened to that lady, I thought it would benefit her life more than mine. I just wanted to try and improve her standard of life. It is a huge amount of money but I've been lucky throughout my life...'

Think of Ten Thousand Whole Pounds and what he might have done with it. This is a world where even Members of Parliament have shown themselves to be as venal as the average Joe who steals office supplies and in which people are judged by what they have and what they wear. Everybody seems to want something for nothing – yet Lloyd was given something for something, and still gave it away. He showed no sense of entitlement, but absolute humility, compassion, generosity and gratitude for his own blessings. Honestly, next time you feel gloomy, think of Lloyd Gardner and remember all the evidence of good.

45

A LESSON FROM A BABY

'I hope you can read this without thinking me a bad, selfish person,'
wrote a mother whose second child was born with Down's syndrome,
and who had (with her husband) decided to have the baby adopted.
'My psychologist calls me brave and honest for admitting how I felt, but I
don't feel brave, just horrible.'

THERE WILL BE readers who judge you as 'bad and selfish'
– perhaps those who have known the love of a child with
Down's syndrome and found their lives blessed by that very
particular affection and their own life-affirming tenderness. They will
find your decision as shocking as it is sad. Yet others will understand
and acknowledge that you have put into words hard truths people
avoid. As for me, I want you to know right away that I will not pass
judgement on a woman who has suffered so much. Your letter was
over twice as long as I have space for – and so I know that you are

racked by guilt and confusion, which gets worse by the day. This is all recent and raw and I feel profoundly sorry for you.

It's interesting that you don't ask me for specific advice. You are worried about your daughter, but a child psychologist has already counselled you how to present the situation to a five-year-old who was looking forward to meeting her baby sister. You must surely have realised that she would probably have been delighted by the baby and been permanently enhanced by her own love and protectiveness. It's impossible for any of us to know what the future will bring, yet you have chosen to imagine the worst (the baby ruining family life) and to act accordingly. It might have been very different – but speculation is pointless. You have made your decision. The issue is how to help you live with it.

Your dread of the judgement of others is an extension of how you judge yourself. I suspect your sense of inadequacy began when you were cheated of the rosy, contented first pregnancy you expected. Your bad experience left you terrified of a second pregnancy, and now it had ended like this. From my personal experience, I know that you are feeling useless at the whole business of having children. Consumed with rage at the hospital as you are, your real anger is at yourself for not being strong and 'big' enough to cope with a Down's baby. So it's absolutely vital that you keep talking to your psychologist and to your husband, in the knowledge that your family has already been changed irrevocably by what has happened and that it must be 'processed' properly and understood.

Your daughter will go on asking questions and perhaps even seek to know her sister – so be prepared for that. Perhaps you will go on to have another child, perhaps not. I wish you and your husband courage in supporting each other in the decision, but suggest gently that another pregnancy would be hazardous to your mental health. Your sheer terror would badly affect your ability to mother that five-year-old who needs you. She won't be an only child if you make your house a warm and welcoming place for all her friends, from now until when she leaves home.

The truth is this – your baby will *always* be present in your life, even though she will be receiving loving care from somebody else. Your first child taught you about love. Your second has taught you the nature of suffering – and I ask you to see that your new quest is to allow that knowledge to help you grow. Now I wish you calm and acceptance and forgiveness – because humility and wisdom reach us through unexpected paths.

To know the world's injustice requires only a small amount of experience. To accept it without bitterness or envy you need almost the sum total of human wisdom...

William Maxwell (1908–2000), *The Folded Leaf* (1945)

46

JUDGEMENT

TWO WEEKS AGO, I answered a letter from an eighteen-year-old having an affair with her former teacher, who was married with a young son. 'Grace' was stuck within her hopeless passion for this older man. She was very, very unhappy and my reply was bracing. I was not unsympathetic; I just wanted her to get away from this damaging situation. And actually, if she doesn't, I foresee a pattern of behaviour that could turn her into a helpless victim, like some of the adults who write to me...

Anyway, one or two readers have told me I was 'harsh' in my reply to Grace, and the dreaded word, 'judgemental', was also used. But a heartbroken mother also wrote, telling me that her daughter left home as soon as she turned eighteen, to move in with a 52-year-old married man who had been in a position of trust, yet having an affair with her for two years. She writes, 'This man has devastated his family and my own by his actions.'

What I want to know is this: how does one stop 'being judgemental' in these cases? I objected to the fact Grace told me that she 'despised' her lover's deceived wife and I made it clear that I do not approve of the situation. Why should I? What right has this child to 'despise' the woman, wife and mother – the innocent human being – she is colluding to deceive?

Similarly, anyone would wonder what kind of man, aged fifty, would start an affair with a sixteen-year-old? Surely sensible and sensitive people can't help making judgements when we feel that somebody is adding to the mess and misery of the world? Professionals in the therapy business have to withhold their views – but you don't, and nor do I.

And during the last few years of writing this column I have actually found that 'talking tough' can be very effective. Many times I have subsequently heard that the reader benefited from the short, sharp verbal slap – and so, when it feels appropriate, I shall go on giving them. This is honest. People get away with the most appalling selfishness – all because they say they're 'in love' and 'can't help it'. And maybe their friends and family respond with a lazy, indulgent 'Oh, you poor thing' or 'We can't control our feelings.'

No. Some of us need to say: Hang on, this is *wrong*.

47

BELIEVE IN SANTA

Y OU CAN HAVE an epiphany in the most unlikely place –
a moment of understanding or insight that lights the day.
Having spent last Sunday morning writing Christmas cards,
we went off to reward ourselves by meeting friends at Bath's scruffy,
'alternative' pub, The Bell. My son used to hang out there as a teenager; all ages and all types congregate in the creatively battered
hostelry – as far from a fashionable gastro-pub as possible and all
the better for it.

Anyway, the local band was called Bill Smarme & The Bizness and
I'd describe them as zany West Country rock with plenty of jokes.
In stage patter about Father Christmas, lead singer Bill pointed out
that when you're young you believe in Father Christmas and when
you get older you don't, but then you become Father Christmas and
then ... well, there were a couple more stages, ending with the fact
that when you're old you *look* like Father Christmas. Everybody gig-
gled because few there were in the first flush of youth.

But I'd stopped listening by then – taken by his point that you *become* Father Christmas. Of course! I thought of all the parents who will be stuffing stockings on Christmas Eve and all those offering carefully wrapped presents to friends and loved ones, and thought how lucky we are to have this yearly feast that focuses on Giving. And let nobody say *that*, in the purest sense, has nothing to do with the true meaning of Christmas. What about the story of the Three Kings?

Then it occurred to me that we can all be guided to a miraculous fourth stage of belief by 'becoming' Father Christmas.

Stage one – the child believes in the magical being.

Stage two – real life as well as age puts paid to that belief.

Stage three – as a mature adult you discover the sublime joy of generosity, so in that sense you are transformed, symbolically, into the jolly, generous bloke in the red kit.

Stage four – with that living proof before you, what else can you do but believe in old Santa all over again?

Yes, and angels too. Happy Christmas.

48

A RIPOSTE TO CYNICS

HAVE YOU MADE some resolutions? Last year mine was to drink less, and I have kept to it. Oh, I still enjoy a glass or three of wine, but I've cut back on the partying and feel better for it. This year I also want to try to make some changes to the way I live, to achieve more peace.

What I've also resolved is to be even more optimistic and trusting than ever. Call me soppy and gullible – and I say, 'Right on!' Make fun of me and I shall chuckle too. Jeer at me for being idealistic and I shall crank up the ideals. Tell me to 'get real' and I shall riposte that all the good things I believe in ARE real. So there.

This is my response to the cynicism I see all around, especially on the internet. I've told you before that I find most online comment poisonous and believe it to be a pollutant in the ether, contributing to global harming. I only make myself read it from time to time because I *should* – since people who write about human emotions have to be aware of their worst aspects. But I hate it.

Anyway, picking up what I wrote recently about taking care of the elderly, some readers have pointed out (correctly) that old people can be vindictive and horrible and deserve to be on their own. But in the horrible *tone* of such comments I detect deep sadness, borne of unhappy childhoods. I know that 'the family' can be a terrible place. But truly I do not need irritating people who revel in their own bitterness to tell me to 'get real'.

Instead, you cynics, tell me this – should you deny the existence of love because you have never experienced it? Do you deny the reality of green because you are colour-blind? Do you assert that Mozart is rubbish because you are deaf? I tell you, if you deny the possibility of hope then you will never achieve any happiness. Why not make a New Year resolution to believe – in spite of yourself – that goodness is possible?

Draw happiness from yourself, from a good day's work,
from the light it brings to the fog that surrounds us.

Henri Matisse (1869–1954), *Jazz* (1947)

49

ANGELS AND SNOWDROPS

Here is a 55-year-old woman, a breadwinner, a trier but lacking in confidence. Worn down by tiredness and problems she 'seems to have lost faith in everything'. Her question is: 'What can I do to sort myself out?'

Y OU KINDLY MENTION my recent long article on angels – which some people interpreted as meaning I actually believe in tall people with long white robes and wings, flying around! In fact, the article closed with a rather different vision, which will make as good a starting point as any. This is what I wrote:

Belief in angels gives the reassurance that there is something 'out there', both powerful and benevolent. We call kind people 'angels', and a loving mother will think nothing of calling her child 'my little angel' – because instinctively we feel that angels represent all goodness, all love. And we need to trust that that they have the

*power to make virtue triumph in the end. That's what my angels
(by that I meant the artworks I have around the house, referred to
in the original piece) are 'for' – and why I believe the song of the
angels is a music that permeates the everyday world: joyful and
consoling. You hear it most of all in the simplest words of kindness
and it accompanies all our moral choices too. Imagine what life
would be like if all people listened acutely.*

The central thought is about human (not divine) love and goodness.

And such consolations are at the heart of your letter, the only
problem being that you have closed your eyes and ears to them. That
may be because your unspecified 'demons' (depression? lack of self-
esteem?) are still working against you, as if to prove the old battles
are never quite over. You compare yourself unfavourably with others who seem more fortunate, yet you have a good kind husband,
two children who are doing well, and the capacity for friendship.
Your grief at the loss of your best friend and your parents (to witness the effects of dementia is to suffer a drawn-out bereavement) is
palpable, and is surely at the root of this current malaise. But 'looking from the outside' (as you request) I ask you to realise that grief
is yet another manifestation of love. Do you see what I'm getting
at? You have much love in your life, and do your best for those you
care for – so must start to pull yourself upwards by recognising the
significance of that. Why not look in the mirror and see a woman
there who deserves the blessings she has? That's a good belief to
bolster you for recovery.

Next, you should face up to the little demons nibbling away at
your capacity for happiness. Dislike of ageing may be one – because
you mention the superiority of younger people at work. Allow them

their language – understanding that yours is just as valuable. Become the one with quiet wisdom they turn to. After all, you have years of experience – so stop fretting about unimportant things. Does a mere 'meeting' mean much, compared with the loss of your friend? Of course not. Use the pain you have suffered to give valuable perspective.

Then again, I fear a part of you may secretly resent your husband for turning you into the main breadwinner. If this is true, you must face up to the thought in order to vanquish it. You must also talk frankly to him about the family finances and see if you really do need to work flat out. Tiredness combined with that undercurrent of grief will hamper your battle with these negative feelings. It would be better if your sons took part-time jobs as well as studying (which thousands do) rather than you should knock yourself out trying to give them financial support. You don't have to compensate for your empty-nest sadness by keeping them dependent.

You must carve out time for yourself when you can follow any hobby (painting?) you fancy. What is stopping you is your own anxiety and this obsession with bolstering yourself through work. If you set aside even one weekend morning to get out the sketch book or tapestry wools, or teach yourself how to bake (one of my own goals for this year!) you will find the activity immensely therapeutic. Oh, what am I saying? You will *enjoy* yourself. And the house won't fall down. On the contrary, your contentment will shore it up.

You say you suspect that something in people's genetic make-up means they can't change. Well, if I believed that I would be incapable of writing this column. Naturally, I agree with your husband that life is tough, but we need to ask – why is it so? My answer is: to test us – and kick-start our capacity for growth.

Outside my study window, the snowdrops have forced their way through a layer of leaf mould so thick you'd think it would crush their fragile green shoots. But no, they are defeating winter. And so can we.

In the deserts of the heart
Let the healing fountain start.

W. H. Auden (Anglo-American poet, 1907–73)

50

PANTOMIME HORSE

This was written after the 2010 general election, as a result of which the Conservative Party led by David Cameron formed a coalition with the Liberal Democrats, led by Nick Clegg.

HERE'S AN OLD Romanian saying to make you think: 'A change of rulers is the joy of fools.' I learned it when I spent time in Romania, researching an adult novel and then one for children, called *The Voices of Silence*. Well, now that British voices have spoken contradictions we've ended up in an intriguing political situation. But I don't use the quote to imply that change is foolish, because I truly believe we needed it, even if this odd, challenging form: a coalition government. No, it's another way of saying that over-optimistic 'tribalism' in politics is foolish and misguided. The mindless chorus of 'things can only get better' rings hollowly in the real world – 'the joy of fools' indeed. Give me low-key, bleakish sincerity that doesn't minimise difficulty.

Yet tribalism is still rife – and as dangerous as the black-and-white approach to human relationships. Which I often discuss in this column. My ex-husband and I had a prominent Labour grandee friend who once opined that it was impossible to understand why we were also friends with Tories. And why? Because of the rank prejudice that says, 'I hate a Tory' – even if that Conservative is the most upright person in the world, and good to his parents too. Ever the pragmatist, I have no time for it. Conviction is all very well, but not if it is resolutely blinkered. Too many passionate Labour supporters I've met seem to want (if they were honest) a one-party state.

This page often bangs on about compromise – and for good reason. It is the only way to conduct a life that is shared (necessarily, unless you are a hermit) with others, with their own feelings, their own needs. In between the blacks and the whites are the many shades of grey I try to deal with. And that's why, strangely, I rejoice at what my colleague Max Hastings has called 'a pantomime horse' in government. Let the prancing rival steeds stay in the stables, neighing and whinnying their protests, while the cobbled-together nag is harnessed to the national cart. Like a true statesman, David Cameron said, 'Real change is when everybody pulls together.' Yes – and a cessation of kneejerk tribalism, in public and personal life, would be the joy of the wise.

AFTER THE AFFAIR

Dear Bel,

After being in a comfortable but unexciting marriage for fourteen years, three years ago I met my soulmate. This lady and I found an immediate rapport. For two and a half years we had a secret but beautiful affair, snatched days and stolen nights. In all that time we had never a cross word or the slightest disagreement and had a fulfilling sex life, sharing many of our most intimate thoughts and memories. I know full well that she loved me but she never told me out loud. We often said that if we'd met in the mid-1980s, we'd have married and the children she had from a previous marriage would have been ours. But a month ago she met another man who offered permanence. She didn't dump me – we met and spoke of this situation at some length and it really hit me hard when she said she wanted to move on. I was devastated because until then I didn't realise just how much she meant to me and how much I loved her. We have parted friends but the loss has caused me more anguish than I ever thought possible. I want to know if you agree with me that you should 'Carpe Diem' – Seize the Day. My message to others is – if you meet your soulmate, don't delay but tell her you love her and set up house together. He who hesitates is lost, as I was – and still am.

Jake

NOW HERE IS an interesting dilemma for me. The lead letter on this page is from 64-year-old 'Dorrie' whose husband left her after twenty-five years, 'because he did not love me any more but wanted somebody else'. I feel nothing but sympathy for that abandoned lady – but what do *you* feel? Perhaps you believe her husband is quite right to put into practice what you are (in effect) preaching and that, therefore, Dorrie just has to put up and shut up. As your own poor wife would have had to have done, if you'd moved out to be with your 'soulmate'.

Yet just contemplate Dorrie's pain and confusion and imagine she is your sister and then ask yourself if the price is too great. But I use the word 'dilemma' because there is, nevertheless, a part of me that understands that when people are deeply in love they *will* hurt others – because that is (I'm afraid) an inescapable part of the human condition. So, do I agree with your philosophy of 'Seize the Day?' It was very much a part of the late '60s to mid-'70s way of thinking that formed me, for better or for worse. It led to many mistakes too, and much heartbreak. So now … I just don't know.

The thing is, Jake, all of us who write advice columns are forced to confront, every single day, the fallout from romantic selfishness. I have no doubt that your letter is preaching to the converted in many cases – since untold numbers of men and women run away from their marriages to shack up with another love. Some of those new relationships last, others don't. Families are hurt and sometimes the ripples from that big stone thrown into the midst of things go on making waves for decades. What is to be done? Illicit love has been a subject of great literature for centuries, and always will be – because the beating of the restless human heart cannot always be stilled.

All I can say to you is this: you have no way of knowing if your relationship with the lady would have lasted even if you *had* thrown away your marriage to be with her. You might have been blissfully happy – or you might have found that even an exciting 'soulmate' loses her shine when exposed to the mundane light of the everyday. So you will do yourself no good by continuing to fantasise about Paradise Lost. You must tuck away your memories in a special 'box' inside your head where you keep precious things, and imagine yourself turning a key.

Now live the life you have – and make it a good one.

She was two divorces down ... both because she had gone off with someone else ... grown into unhappiness because she did not realise that happiness came from sticking at things – things that often seemed mundane, prosaic, boring, unglamorous.

Alexander McCall Smith (b. 1948), *The Uncommon Appeal of Clouds* (2012)

*The important thing, the thing that lies before me,
the thing that I have to do ... is to absorb into my nature
all that has been done to me, to make it a part of me,
to accept it without complaint, fear, or reluctance.*

Oscar Wilde (1854–1900), *De Profundis* (1897)

52

PURPOSE AFTER LOSS

People often call it the worst of griefs. This lady's daughter died two years earlier, aged six, from a 'devastating degenerative condition'. The little girl gave her purpose and 'now she's gone I feel so abandoned. It's the most frightening thing to feel so lonely. I can deal with the grief – but not this.' The question: 'Is this what happens to all people who've lost a child – do they lose their friends too? Is it because nobody can understand how it changes you?'

YOUR LONG CRY from the heart ran over eight handwritten pages, untold grief behind each line. It's terrible to imagine you reaching for the telephone to talk to a bereavement helpline, to no avail. Since I often recommend specific telephone helplines (like the Child Death Helpline or The Compassionate Friends) I should point out that usually they can't possibly have the funding to operate all hours. They would if they could. But I want everybody to know that the marvellous Samaritans do, and in despair you can ring them on 08457 909090.

People have asked me in the past if it is possible to 'get over' the death of a child and I want to reply – can we ever stop the rain from falling, or our days slipping forward into night? Of course things don't 'get easier' and you are right to be frustrated because the people around you seem to think you should have 'moved on' – or whatever glib phrase they may choose. The pain you feel (over what is surely the worst of all the losses that may have to face) will always be there, beating like a vein under the surface of your skin forever. I don't say that to make you feel worse (how would that be possible?) but because one of my own philosophies is that we should not expect to 'get over' any of the losses that are a part of being human. On the contrary, I believe that we honour our beloved dead by carrying our losses with us, just as a snowball rolls along picking up snow. In time, and with the right help, that process can add to the sum total – the spiritual size, if you like – of who we are.

Yet, in order for this to take place we have to learn to accept what has happened. It's not a question of forgetting our grief, but of processing it, so that we can allow it to help us grow. Two years on, you are barely at the beginning of that particular journey. There is much talk about the 'stages of grief' and indeed the nature of it does change – but who is to stipulate how long that may take? For six years you took care of a child who needed everything from you. Although you have other children, you say that your daughter's care gave you 'purpose'. Within that sentence there are so many questions I don't have room to unpick – but I do beg you now to see that your purpose as a mother still goes on, each day, within your home.

Let's think about your friends now. In your longer letter you expressed great anger with them, and so I want to point out – very gently – that in some ways I agree with your husband. You are expecting too much. Yes, they do 'owe' you something – they owe you sensitivity. But people are often terrified to face up to the depths of a friend's loss because it is an all-too-vivid reminder of the bereavements they will have to face themselves and of their own mortality. 'I just don't know what to say' is a common response, but I want you to see it as helpless, not mean-spirited or callous. Forgive them – because they don't know what they are doing to you.

You say your daughter's life and care gave you 'the greatest purpose' – and that you wanted to turn that to good use by choosing to work with special needs children. Now although I applaud that motivation, surely you are expecting far too much of yourself, rather as you expect too much from those around you? It is not for us to *plan* what long-term use we will be able to make of the pain that has afflicted us. No, we must wait for the universe to unfold that purpose. Which is a way of suggesting that perhaps you should leave the demanding job that surely makes it very hard (if not impossible) for you to come to terms with your daughter's destiny, and all the questions it raised in your heart.

Last, let me ask you not to see your husband as 'annoyed' or your friends as lacking 'compassion'. Your friends do care for you but retreat (quite naturally) within their own lives, their own problems. Your husband has his own grief to deal with, so don't push him away. You are *not* alone, Linda. Let your immediate family support you – by taking on the noble task of supporting them. With your daughter's brave little spirit in mind, make this your new purpose.

There is a hollow space too vast for words
Through which we pass with each loss,
Out of whose darkness we are
sanctioned into being.

Rashani Réa (poet)

53

BRAVE DAUGHTER

Sometimes a letter arrives that really resonates, giving me hope. So it was
with Renee – telling me about her daughter:

'About eighteen months ago, she started dating a man she first met some
years before. He had just come out of his second failed relationship. They
got engaged recently with the most romantic of proposals, and planned
an autumn wedding. They wanted to start a family soon after and he was
adamant that they should live in the country to provide the same upbringing
she'd had, even near to me (for babysitting) as he knew that was what she
would like. She was so happy, looking forward to her dream wedding to the
man she adored and a cottage in the country – garden, children and pets.
Then a month ago he sent her a text saying it was all over, switched his
phone off and ignored her calls.

She was devastated. Absolutely distraught. Back home for a few days she
tried to understand what had just happened. She knew in her heart it was
final as it was such a cruel, cowardly action that spoke volumes of what he

could be capable of. She told me to cancel everything and then dipped into the 'wedding fund' to get her hair done and book a flight to visit a friend on a Greek island. She has put her flat up for sale, saying she needs a project and intends to buy that house with a garden. If she can't do it with him – she'll do it without him! I know inside she's truly shattered and I ache for her. But I want to pay tribute to the brave and beautiful daughter I'm so proud of.'

YOU OFTEN SEND me anecdotes and comments, and sadly I rarely have room to print them – although I always love reading these personal communications. But I hope this story will remind those in a similar situation that you really do have to 'pick yourself up, dust yourself off and start all over again' – as that chirpy song from my childhood says. There's no choice. I also love the fact that this proud (but angry and upset) mother chose to share it. With such a family behind her, the young woman – so cruelly jilted – will triumph in the end.

54

'WORLD'S WORST BASTARD'?

Dear Bel,

I am sixty-four with two daughters and three grand-daughters. I married my wife forty-two years ago, but shortly before our ruby anniversary I noticed subtle changes that became progressively worse. She was diagnosed with Alzheimer's, became increasingly irrational and was eventually admitted to the local hospital's psychiatric unit and then to residential care. I was devastated and so were our daughters ... Now I have become close to one of my clients, a widow my age ...Rracked with guilt, I feel I have betrayed my wife, who I still love. I am not proud of myself for getting into this situation as I still love my wife ... Our daughters were not happy, but say life is short and if I am happy, so be it. I am not looking for absolution (although I did consider talking to a local vicar, then rejected the thought) but simply an unbiased outside opinion. Am I the world's worst bastard or a victim of circumstance?

I N THE CHRISTIAN church absolution means forgiveness for sins committed – and although you say this is not what you want, it seems to me obvious that you do. The standard prayer begins, 'Almighty God who forgives all who truly repent, have mercy on you, pardon and forgive you…' You may not choose to express your own feelings in religious terms, and yet at a very deep level you need to be told that you are forgiven by a force outside yourself. Because you need to help you forgive yourself.

In truth, I cannot imagine anybody judging you as 'the world's worst bastard'.

If you were to enter a Roman Catholic confessional you might well be told to 'go and sin no more' but I believe that the majority of readers will agree with your daughters. And they are the only ones with the right to judge this sad case.

You stoutly maintain that you still love the wife with whom you shared a long married life, but the painful fact is this: that wife is no longer with you. One of the cruellest aspects of dementia is that those who love the sufferer are left bereaved – condemned to witness what is, after all, a form of living death. You do not say whether your wife still recognises you, but since it sounds as if the progress of the disease was cruelly fast, I fear it may be unlikely. Devastated, you kept going, and then met another lonely person who could offer mental and physical comfort. Which (I have no doubt) is as important for her as it is for you.

Honestly, Peter, I can only find it in my heart to be happy that you have found solace with your lady friend. The wife you loved will never come home to you, but you could read a really useful book by

Oliver James called *Contented Dementia*, which will perhaps give you some ideas about ways to enjoy the times you have with her. Your visits are important for both of you (and for your daughters) and nothing should get in their way. As for the rest of the time … Well, when something is lost the universe often supplies something to be found – and bring joy.

The artist ... speaks to our capacity for delight and wonder, to the sense of mystery surrounding our lives; to our sense of pity, and beauty, and pain; to the latent feeling of fellowship with all creation.

Joseph Conrad (Polish author, 1857–1924)

55

TOY STORY

YOU KNOW THAT feeling when a work of art just lifts you? It might be a beloved piece of music, or a book, or standing in front of a picture and losing yourself in its colour and texture. All three mean so much to me. But this week I enjoyed an artistic transformation equal to any. We went to see *Toy Story 3*.

There we were in the cinema at half past five, looking rather silly in our chunky black £1 3D specs, waiting eagerly for the antics of Woody, Buzz, Mr and Mrs Potato Head and the gang to work their magic. Naturally, we already knew the first two movies. The layers of reference have to be appreciated, not to mention the sheer comic invention of the whole.

Some of you might be thinking that I'm going mad – to wax so lyrical over a computer-generated animation about a bunch of talking toys. But no – any parent who has choked up at the looming reality of a beloved son or daughter leaving home will respond. Anybody who believed a beloved toy was real will understand. Anybody who has ever felt overwhelmed about the big life changes that affect us all will be moved. Anybody who has ever been delighted by the evidence of a friend's loyalty will understand. Any soldier (or team-mate) who has known about the importance of comradeship will take a deep breath. Any teacher or parent who sees what imaginative play can do for a child will smile and say 'Yes!' Any woman who has realised that her man is less than she thinks he is – but accepts and loves him all the same – will understand (Oh, Barbie and Ken!). Anybody with the heart to see how rejection can corrode the soul (Oh, Lotso!) will be moved to tears. As I was. Towards the end, great boiling droplets ran down my cheeks.

Toy Story 3 offers laughter, thrills and real hope, at a time when they are sorely needed. Come to think of it, they are *always* needed. See it – do.

56

HE'S LEAVING HOME

This lady is already suffering because her 'quiet lad' is going to university:
'How will he cope as he can't cook, despite me trying to teach him the
basics? I wake at night and worry ... I don't know how to deal with these
feelings that something dreadful will happen if I let him out of my sight.
What do I have to do?'

T HERE IS NO easy way to answer – other than to point out
that the reality of your son going away will be even worse
than the imaginary pain you are enduring, and there is nothing you can do about it. Does that sound too blunt? If so, I can't help
it – because you simply have to accept this stage as something to be
experienced, endured and overcome. Yes, you knew I was going to
say that! I picked your letter out because you are quite right: this is
a universal problem for many parents at this time of year, whether
their offspring are going to university right away, or perhaps taking

a gap year. Actually some mothers feel anguish when their children leave primary school. That's another parting, like the first day at nursery. All these stages have to be faced.

When your child reaches eighteen you have to understand that you are marooned on a pretty uncomfortable wall, looking both ways at once. One side of you suspects what older mothers (like myself) are already experiencing: that you go on being a mother even when your children grow up, marry etc. The other side hankers back for the time of childhood ('it was so much easier') and must come to terms with the fact that when your children grow you have to let them go.

It sounds as if it is a bit harder for you, simply because your son is so well-behaved! I've often thought that nature turns teenagers into fearsome monsters as a means of helping their parents welcome their departure. Yet here we have a mum cross-examining her son's friends about whether he's so quiet he will bore them. Extraordinary! As well as mistaken. That's the sort of fussing that can alienate a young adult, never mind the friends. You must take a firm hold of yourself now – before this irrational worrying upsets both men in your life. In your longer letter you say your house 'will be like a morgue' when your son leaves. Well, only if you give up the ghost. Your son may be the most important element in your life, but I wouldn't reveal that to your husband, if I were you.

You write, 'This is me' with no explanation. I take it to mean that you have always lived for and through your son. You also write, 'He is mine.' Well, actually he is not yours. His life is his own. May I suggest that you do an internet search for 'Kahlil Gibran+children' and read what you find there – or, better still, buy the book *The Prophet*. Think of your son as the messenger you are sending forth into the future and make sure his journey is as easy and unburdened as possible. If you don't get a grip on your emotions, he may stay away. If you control yourself, he will want to come back.

Your children are not your children.
They are the sons and daughters of Life's longing for itself.
They come through you but not from you,
And though they are with you, yet they belong not to you.

Kahlil Gibran (Lebanese–American artist and poet, 1883–1931)

Everyone is alone at the heart of the earth,
Pierced by a ray of sunlight:
And suddenly it's evening.

Salvatore Quasimodo (Italian author and poet, 1901–68)

57

LOVE IN A LIFE

A s you all know, I receive many letters to this page and very much appreciate the ones that make warm comments, without asking for any help. It touches me that so many of you find it uplifting and instructive to read about the lives of other people.

And from time to time I open a letter that brings tears to my eyes. Like this one. Written in biro on lined file paper, it has no address – and no name either. This is what it says:

Dear Bel,

You have a lot of trouble and heartache to deal with in your profession. So just for a change I would like to tell you a lovely story. I met my wife when I was seventeen and she was sixteen. It was in the '40s at the church dance (sixpence to get in on Wednesday and ninepence on Sunday). I had seen her on many occasions but she was so pretty that I didn't think I had a chance because plenty of lads were chasing her and I was just ordinary. This particular night a lad was bothering her so I went over and told him to lay off. The next dance was a ladies' choice and – I couldn't believe my luck – my dream girl walked across to me and asked me to dance. I took her home and we started courting. I married her three years later and we had four children. At Christmas 2009 we celebrated sixty years of married life – then, just one month later, my wife died. I miss her so much. But I was so lucky. I married my Dream and we had sixty wonderful years and four wonderful children. As a Christian I believe we will be reunited – and I am waiting.

This lovely man adds, 'I don't expect you to publish this. It's for you.'

But I can't resist sharing this little beacon of light, as an antidote to all the bad news that afflicts us most days. I am so grateful to my reader for reminding us that love can be more powerful than death.

58

MY BROTHER

FROM TIME TO time I write about bereavement on this page, because it is part of the pattern of all our lives and can never be forgotten – much as we naturally push death from our minds. No advice column should only deal with love and sex, for loss takes many forms and sometimes I feel that all the sorrows we experience along the way are but rehearsals for the big one – the sudden absence of someone who's always been there.

For years I've quietly made this one of my interests and was honoured to be given an award by the marvellous charity Cruse (presented by the Queen as their patron) for articles about bereavement. That was back in 1984.

But now I am bereaved myself and – like everybody else – struggle to make sense of mortality. You can read countless books and write words for others, but then you face it yourself. Deep breath. As you get older you expect people you care about to die, but that doesn't make it any less of a shock. In March, I wrote about my brother, celebrating his sixty-sixth after years of suffering. I told how he had (only just) survived a terrible car smash at the age of nineteen and spent years in hospital. He was told he would never even make it to a wheelchair but his indomitable spirit triumphed and when he married Bev in 1976 he was leaning on just one stick. We were all awestruck by what he managed to make of his life, against the odds. And by the way, the NHS served him magnificently.

Still, recent years have been very tough indeed. He was housebound and in pain and his body was beginning to say 'That's enough.' So I can only give thanks that he left us in an instant, in his own home, with two lovely carers at his side. And I choose to remember William and me happily playing Monopoly, chucking snowballs and tumbling together down the sand dunes at Ainsdale, Lancashire, when we were children, and all life lay ahead.

In the depth of winter I finally learned that within me there lay an invincible summer.

Albert Camus (French author and philosopher, 1913–60)

59

A SORRY SAGA

A husband is unfaithful. His wife vows revenge, then she is unfaithful and walks out on husband and two teenage girls. Then her relationship breaks up but meanwhile her ex has remarried. Now her eldest daughter has a baby that 'Maggy' is not allowed to see. 'The only person for me is my ex-husband and I'd give anything to have him and my family life back. Why is it so difficult to move on? Believe me I've tried, but no one really understands the pain I feel.'

THE QUESTION I need first to ask is this: Do *you* understand the pain you feel?

By that I mean – really, truly understand what caused it? An outsider might feel rather sorry for you, knowing that it is in the nature of human beings to make terrible mistakes, to wish they had not done so, and then find that the river has flowed onwards with a current too strong to turn back. This is the human condition. Yet your letter to me is oddly – even irritatingly – blank, as if you have only a slim understanding of cause and effect. The proof is in that extraordinary statement, 'to this day I do not know why,' followed by the naïve question, 'why does my daughter hate me so much?' Your current pain seems entirely for yourself; nowhere do I detect real remorse for the heartbreak you inflicted on your family.

Truly, it gives me no pleasure to be harsh, but I have to ask if you realise that actions have consequences? Let everybody reading this take heed. The sad story of what happened to this one family is all too common, I'm afraid.

First, your husband was unfaithful. You bided your time, nursing poisonous thoughts of revenge, then finally skipped out and 'devastated' the family. But your ex wasn't so 'devastated' that he couldn't turn around and move a strange woman into the home within three months. Speedy or what? To explain that to the teenagers would have taken some doing, so I can only guess that he stoked their hostility towards you – a rage that stemmed from his deep hurt at abandonment. In the meantime, you ditched the new love (another damaged person in the sorry saga?) because you decided you still wanted the lovely familiar toys that you'd thrown out of the pram.

No matter how happy your ex might be now, your daughters will always blame you for breaking up the family life they knew. You must understand that. Nothing to be done but accept the consequence of what you did. The first step towards making things better (and oh … that misleading phrase 'move on'…) would be for you to stop offering excuses (there are always plausible reasons for us to do bad things) and acknowledge that you caused your children terrible pain. And are still paying. That's how it was – and is. Yes, of course I would want your daughters to forgive you – but people should understand that forgiveness is one of the hardest things to achieve. And sometimes impossible – like many great goods.

Unless you can stop hankering for the past you will not be able to form any new relationship – as you have found. Remember that your husband was unfaithful first and wasted no time in finding a new woman. I say that not to make you continue to justify yourself, but in order that you'll face the future realistically. Admit that you did a wrong thing, but he had too – and in order to punish him you lost him. Acknowledge that therefore the sadness you feel is (despite what he did) your own fault, take some deep breaths, and let him go from your mind. Finally, I hope that you let your two daughters know how truly repentant you are now – not how *miserable* but how *sorry* – and that in time the elder one will soften towards you and allow you to be a grandmother. Your bitter jealousy of their stepmother ('I can't bear her to be called Grandma') may be understandable, but it's pointless. You left a hole in their lives and she filled it. It's now up to you to fill the hole in your *own* life with honesty, humility and hope.

You shall ask me,
What good are dead leaves?
And I will tell you:
They nourish the sore earth.

Nancy Wood (American author, b. 1936)

60

FOX

I T WAS THREE in the afternoon and my mind was focused on writing the column, when I heard a distant commotion outside my ground-floor study window – and knew something was wrong. Our hens roam freely about the garden all day, clucking in their gentle silly way, but this time squawks of sheer terror penetrated my preoccupation. I jumped up – to see the young fox almost upon our feathered girls.

Flinging open the window, I bellowed, somewhat bizarrely, 'Hoi! hoi! hoi!' (What primitive depths did that come from?) and he fled as quickly as he'd come. But as the weather gets colder, foxes, like all living things, become desperate to survive. So he or she will be back, for certain. And if somebody shoots him, his relatives will still view our place as fast food central.

There's nothing to be done. People who don't let their chickens out know that hungry foxes can tunnel under a fence. Even urban folk find their hens slaughtered by bold foxes. And since we have a tiny white dog, I'm also uncomfortably aware that large male foxes have been known to attack small dogs – although normal-sized canine companions are their natural enemy. So we'll keep an eye on Bonnie and try to look out for the chickens, and that's all we can do.

It makes me realise how ludicrously flawed is the whole concept of 'rights' in a context like this. Animal rights fanatics have made it clear they value the life of a fox above that of a human baby (remember the case of the fox who crept into a house?) but they never explain how they feel about the 'right' of the poor hens to wander happily foraging and providing us (and our young neighbours) with delicious eggs. Or the 'rights' of the mallards and other wild creatures who will certainly fall foul of Mr Fox on his quest to feed himself and his family. Which – naturally – he has every 'right' to do.

When you live in the countryside, keep animals and love to watch wildlife, you know it's all as complicated as the problems I deal with on this page.

61

WHERE IS THE HAPPY FAMILY?

Here is a girl whose father died one month earlier (from an intentional overdose) and whose mother is engaged to a new partner, making her feel left out: 'I've been replaced … I'm sick of selfish adults who say they love me but never put me first. My childhood was (obviously) far from idyllic and I'm worried I will do the same to my children, not knowing any different … I just want happiness and I don't know how to achieve it. Does the happy family I want even exist for me?'

As this is my last column before Christmas, I'm determined to bring you good tidings of comfort and joy – even though, just now, wintry winds blow cold. Here you are, still only seventeen, and already carrying more burdens than some shoulder in a lifetime. I wish you were here so I could give you a massive hug and tell you that, if you hold fast to your private inner self, things will get better for you. When my daughter was a troubled teenager, ill with a congenital condition, I used to tell her that everything she was going through would be useful one day. Ouch – you should have heard her response to that!

But now, at thirty, she admits I was right. The sorrows she endured have turned her into a wonderful person, with the wisdom to help others. So, I'm asking you, a bright and literate girl, to look at ALL your experiences as an intricately woven magic carpet that will transport you into your future.

You witnessed your parents' unhappiness, your father's deterioration, and now – so recently – you've had the shock of his suicide, with all the complicated feelings of grief, guilt and regret that came with it. Not to mention the wistfulness that family life might have been so different. Meanwhile, the mother you supported has found a man, and blithely put her own happiness ahead of the natural love and sensitivity any mum should show her child. I can't believe they chose a new house without including you ... But there you are, Ashley, it happened. So now you have to make what you can of the hand you've been dealt. All of us must, because there is no choice. To change the metaphor, you can't drop the ball thrown at you – but must run with it, even if the going is tough.

I want you to see your life as a series of stages. At the moment you're full of sadness, which is entirely natural. Soon you'll be at the next phase, and it's vital that you get right away from your mother and her fiancé and do that English degree – even though they are not encouraging. Take a part-time job – whatever it takes. Maybe get away backpacking for a few months too. An English degree is not 'useless', but a passport to many things – but anyway, you don't have to think about that now. Just read as much as you can – and please keep a journal. Write down all your thoughts and feelings every day, because it will help, and also copy out passages you've read that throw light on your feelings. Think of your life as a writer does – as a work in progress. Something for you to create.

There is no reason to assume your dream of a 'happy family' is unattainable. If you didn't learn it at your mother's knee you can learn it at other knees. There are many ways of living, and all the good things and good people in this world are waiting to teach you, Ashley. Trust me, you will find comfort in friends and in older people who'll take an interest in you and (one day) in a man who will love you. You will find it in the blossom each spring, in glorious sunsets, in birdsong – not to mention small acts of kindness from strangers. All this you are walking forward to meet. Hooray!

Believe me, happiness is not something you 'achieve' like A-level results. It would be better to stop worrying about it. Just be excited about the infinite, independent possibilities that await you and stride to meet them.

All situations can be used to deepen our understanding and the sense of magic and beauty in our experiences.

Jack Kornfield (America Buddhist teacher, b. 1945)

62

THE ANCESTOR EFFECT

YOUNGER PEOPLE TEND to hate it when we oldies say things like, 'Oh, when I was growing up we had no central heating, so the inside of the windows iced up.' They probably read the subtext quite correctly: 'So quit moaning and go put on a sweater!'

But, to be serious, I do think it's helpful to realise that we're spoilt and that our grandparents and great-grandparents would think our lives truly cushy. In the '30s poverty meant having no shoes and just bread on the table; now it means circumstances that may seem hard for those experiencing them, but which would be luxurious to a young man on the Western Front in 1916.

The comparison may seem flippant – yet I was fascinated to read of a report just published in the *European Journal of Social Psychology* that says otherwise. Researchers have discovered that thinking about what your ancestors endured can actually help you complete a task or deal with a stressful situation. At a very simple level, you may complain about your kitchen and long for a new, smarter one. So look at pictures of the kitchens of the '50s, or of the nineteenth-century and earlier, and consider the delicious (or at least, nutritious) meals they cooked in them. Your great-grandmother would consider what you have the height of style and convenience, wouldn't she? That's definitely worth thinking about. Do you really need to update?

They say the 'ancestor effect' works because it reminds the brain that seemingly impossible hurdles can be overcome by us modern softies, if we really try – just as they were by people who, after all, shared a similar genetic make-up. That's why I think that all schools should have regular visits from pensioners who can tell kids what it was like to go into a factory at fourteen, or experience London in the blackout with sirens wailing, or make do with rations to feed a family. Even my generation could tell today's young teachers what it was like to be in a class of *fifty* baby boomers and actually do well.

Yes – and that takes me back to, 'Quit moaning!'

63

MY OLD LOVE

This thirty-year-old woman can't get over her break-up with her fiancé. The relationship was making both of them unhappy, but now she is with somebody else, she finds herself dreaming of her ex: 'It seems that coming to terms with our break-up is harder now than ever, and I really don't want to carry regrets around for the rest of my life. What do you think I should do?'

THERE'S A BEAUTIFUL poem by the Chilean poet Pablo Neruda called 'Tonight I Can Write the Saddest Lines', which is about how hard it is to move yourself forward at the end of a great love. (Why not Google that poem now?) The poet recalls his love when it is all over, admitting, 'I no longer love her, that's certain. But perhaps I love her. / Love is so short, forgetting is so long.' Two more lines might offer a glimpse into the heart of your problem: 'Because through nights like this one I held her in my arms / My soul is not satisfied that it has lost her.' With exquisite melancholy

Neruda mourns the death of love, but acknowledges that what happens between two people will never entirely be finished. As your letter demonstrates.

Do you see what I mean? The strange 'grief' you are still feeling is for all the hopes you had, all the wonderful lovemaking you shared through nights, that intense and beautiful intimacy and happiness ... before it all went wrong. You feel intense wistfulness for five years lost – out of your still-young life. But those years were not wasted, they were spent. And while they have left you with nothing but memories to show for good times and bad – all the love, the non-communication and the sadness – they have helped to create the person you are today.

I want you to understand that feelings of regret are entirely normal. Of course, many people want to wipe the dust of their old loves from their feet and leap forward weightlessly into the future. But most of us walk on slowly, always encumbered by feelings, and the knowledge of love that can never be forgotten. That's how I feel about my first marriage, and unbidden tears will still take me by surprise – but I've learned to live with it. A secret, innermost voice will always ask whether you could have tried harder, waited a while longer, clung on a bit more desperately ... I know mine does. But what is the point, now? As Neruda puts it, 'We, of that time, are no longer the same.' Yes, but still – the love we mourn was, for a while, the truest thing in the history of humankind.

You say you don't wish 'to carry regrets around' but I suggest you flip that thought and see your memories not as something to weigh you down, but to enrich you. Rather as if they were carbonised into a single, big, fat diamond. Everything that you shared with that man (good and bad) is an essential part of your life-learning, and should be celebrated for that.

But you know perfectly well (as clearly as anybody reading your letter will see) that your fiancé was far from being your soulmate. How could he have been, when he didn't want to talk to you about the things most precious to you? When he wouldn't listen? You admit, 'There was only sexual intimacy; he wasn't really interested in anything I enjoyed nor in some of the bigger questions of life.' The key phrase is 'good friends or a real team'. Once you have felt that about a partner you realise that it's the most important part of a relationship.

Sometimes you meet a couple who seem mismatched (maybe she's a high-flier and he doesn't have a degree, or he's dynamic and she's a mouse) yet their 'connection' can be truly miraculous. After all, sexual attraction can wane (as you discovered) but if you have true companionship, that is not necessarily a tragedy. Kindness, gentleness, fun, sharing, attention, devotion, silliness, heart-searching … you want all those things, don't you? Well, I hope you have them with your new man, and realise that your ex helped you to define what you need in a partner. So be thankful.

I had not yet learned that we make our own destiny, it springs from within us. It is not the outward events but what we allow ourselves to make of them that count.

Susan Hill (b. 1942), *Mrs de Winter* (1993)

64

ADVICE TO SELF

A YEAR AGO, we moved house. Had you told me then that twelve months on two parts of the home would still be a mess, with boxes still unpacked (because the woodwork is not done) I swear I'd have run away. It was all hard going and I confess that for two or three months (at least) I was very, very miserable, and thought we'd made a terrible mistake. ('Too late,' intoned my husband, with his no-frills approach to emotional issues!)

Looking back over the year, I recognise how much of my gloom could have been dispelled by action. This is what I often advise, isn't it? You know – get up and do this or that and remake your life. Look forward, not back. Don't mope – act. And so on. But do I take my own advice? Of course not! This reminds me of an old Latin tag, '*Quis custodiet custodes?*' which translates: 'Who guards the guards?' Its significance is specific and terrible when we think of cases where a politician has been assassinated by a bodyguard.

But there's a broader meaning for life in general, very relevant to this column in particular: who looks after those who look after? In my own case I could ask, 'Who advises the advice columnist?' Perhaps you, like me, have met medical professionals who totally neglect their own health. Or a couples' counsellor whose own marriage is on the rocks. I once met a garden designer whose own garden was a patch of lawn with a few scrubby shrubs – which told the whole story of her long, drawn-out divorce from a bully. Knowing quite well that gardening can be excellent therapy, she could not apply that wisdom to herself.

Does any of this resonate with you? It's very easy to lay down the law about how others should behave, yet fail to look in the mirror and ask ourselves if we practise what we preach. But, 'Don't do as I do, do as I say' is a complacent get-out I'm determined not to use in the future. Today my advice to this frustrated, complaining advice columnist is brisk: 'Get off your bottom, clear that room at last, and then you'll have done something to make yourself feel better.'

65

LONG AFFAIR

So – twenty-five years ago this lady fell for a married man. Five years later she married, briefly ended the affair, then went back to it. She distanced herself from friends, 'in order to be ready to drop everything if he wanted to see me'. A few months before writing to me she ended the affair – and took out her anger on her suspicious husband. She writes:

'Now my ex-lover Andrew is terrified I will confess all, and he will lose everything. Today I'm angry with him but also with myself for loving him so long with nothing much in return. I feel stupid I didn't figure out he didn't give a damn about me and just used me when he wanted sex. Our spouses have been hoodwinked for over twenty years without having a clue. How the hell do I start again?'

I t is with no disrespect to your problem that I tell you I'm writing while listening to Rod Stewart's CD *Soulbook*. Usually I play quiet classical music to help my thoughts, but today I'm wallowing in that voice (fine-grade steel wool) singing the old songs: 'If You Don't Know Me By Now', 'Tracks of My Tears', 'Rainy Night in Georgia' and so on. A great soundtrack for the universal drama of love, joy and broken hearts – 'It's the Same Old Song'. You know all about that, don't you?

You would not have ditched all your friends, the more easily to be ready for snatched moments with your lover, if you hadn't also feared their judgement. Show me a woman who has thrown away the best years of her life on a married lover and I will show you one condemned by a regiment of head-shaking chums. But add into that mix a woman who made a convenient marriage while in love with somebody else – and then deceived that hard-working husband for over twenty years … well, then, I'm sorry, the chorus of damnation will be swelled by countless men who'll damn you for being a cheat.

Some people will accuse me of being harsh; after all, you wrote asking for help. But it's important that you acknowledge how great a part you have played in your own downfall, before you can clean this mess from your shoes and step forward into the next part of your life.

Oh what a lot of trouble 'love' causes! You were a single mum when you fell for this man, and then he became an addiction. Once 'the internet came in' you could 'talk' up to twenty times a day – and so your habit was fed like that of any junkie. Your lover called all the shots, but you put up with that because of your passion. It was ever thus: as the song goes, 'You really got a hold on me'. You're far from being the first or last person led astray by passion – and to those who condemn you I will just whisper, 'Be glad it never happened to you.' I tell you from experience, it's a sweet pain made worse by shame.

The only advice I can give you is not to deny that this Andrew ever loved you. That will just double your pain and anger – and I don't believe it's true. If you allow yourself to think that you have thrown away half your life on a man who 'didn't give a damn' about you but 'used' you for sex, you will never forgive yourself – or him. You'll probably end up confessing all and driving your husband to tell Andrew's wife … and then that mess on your shoes will be wiped all over innocent people. Which will do no good at all. You have to be very, very strong right now and put on an Oscar-worthy performance for that poor, worried husband of yours. Is it possible to get away on a holiday together? You mention that he likes to watch porn – so suggest he leaves the laptop behind and renews his acquaintance with your own lap. I know you don't *want* this – but it's your only chance of putting things right. You've been acting for a long time, and this is no time to stop.

Listen to me. Andrew did love you. The relationship was not meaningless. Yes, he wanted his cake and ate it too – but that's a human failing, not a crime against humanity. It would do you good to have some counselling to help you pick your way through past, present and future. Possibly your marriage will not survive without the prop of that third person. But for now, don't deny what the past really meant in order to seek justification for behaving badly. Maybe you were wrong – but an illicit love can deserve the name of love, all the same.

Love does not consist in gazing at each other,
but in looking together in the same direction.

Antoine de Saint-Exupéry (French writer and poet, 1900–44)

66

ABJECT

Here is a woman (mid-thirties) locked into a 'relationship' with a vile man who will not work, spends his dole on drugs, is indulged by his mother, watches TV all day while she works, insists on sex 'when he hasn't washed for days', was put on probation for 'trashing the house and attacking me' etc. She ends: 'I want to leave but he says he'll destroy everything and leave me with nothing. I've worked so hard doing up the house and now isn't the time to sell. Also where would my pets go? Why do I stay with him?'

THIS APOLOGY FOR a person is threatening to leave you with 'nothing' if you walk out – but I beg you to confront the truth: that your whole life is one colossal Nothing as long as you are foolish enough to remain in your prison. I read a letter like yours with disbelief. Women with children stay trapped in bad marriages because leaving is so complicated, while older people reach the stage when stepping out alone is too terrifying. But you aren't even forty yet and have no children; therefore there is no reason for you to spend another day with this disgusting man – a violent, dirty, lazy, arrogant, drug-taking, sexist, thieving waste of space who was spoilt by his stupid, indulgent mother and deserves not one second of any self-respecting woman's time.

Why do you stay?

Because you are weak.

I don't want to show zero sympathy. Women in your situation become ground down and afraid. I understand that. But accepting an intolerable situation for the sake of 'a quiet life' (which is far from quiet) is not an option. Don't talk to me about your pets or house prices. Those are peripheral issues. If you have three dogs and a ferret and a snake in a tank you have to get rid of them and save your own life. At the moment the quality of your life is less than that of a beloved family pet, so for heaven's sake don't be sentimental. And it may not be the best time to sell a property, but what could be worse than living as you are? Battered wives who leave everything behind and seek refuge in a shelter show more courage than you. If you were to tell me that you still love this bastard despite yourself then I would at least have a little more understanding than I do. But you don't love him. You despise him – and the longer you stay, the more you will despise yourself for doing so.

On the other hand, we should ask why you should be the one to leave the home to which he makes no contribution. Whether you leave or force him to leave, you cannot do nothing.

First, ignore your feeling of isolation and go to your family and old friends for help. I bet you'll be surprised by their encouragement. Take the boldest path and decide you are going to kick him out of the house. Stay calm and make plans. Next time he is sleeping off one of his drug benders, pack all his things (including the Xbox) and deliver the stuff to his mother. Tell her it's over and warn her seriously that you have some tough friends (no matter if this is a fib) who are going to protect you from her son and so, for the sake of his health and safety, she should advise him to come back home with her. Get advice (Citizens Advice Bureau – or a solicitor) about seeking a restraining order against him. Tell his probation officer he has threatened you, and ask him to tell the police. Change the locks. Preferably do all the above in one day, to daze him with the speed of your attack. He will kick up rough, of course, but this is the time to stand your ground. I hope you can persuade at least one friend or family member to stay with you while this is going on. This man is an inadequate failure and a bully, and such types will usually cave in when they are defied.

If this plan fails then you will have to leave. You have only one life – and the rest of it lies before you. Truly, it would be better for you if he were to burn the house down than to remain in this abject condition.

So between the skies, the river and the hills, generation after generation learnt not to mourn overmuch what the troubled waters had borne away. They entered into the philosophy of the town: that life was an incomprehensible marvel, since it was incessantly wasted and spent, yet none the less it lasted and endured...

Ivo Andrić (1892–1975), *The Bridge on the Drina* (1945)

67

AN OLD LETTER

SORTING THROUGH SOME old papers the other day I came across a letter I'd completely forgotten about. Many years ago, I found it tucked in an old piece of furniture picked up second hand. I kept it carefully, but two house moves buried it once more. The only information on the document is a place and date: Peking 26.5.31. There's a small coat of arms embossed on the paper, but the signature is illegible. I always thought the writer must be a diplomat.

What matters is that the spidery handwriting reveals an affectionate letter from a father to a daughter. It starts, endearingly, 'Well, Margherita old girl, you seem to have been and gone and done it this time.' She has obviously written to tell him that she is engaged to a cavalry officer and the wedding will be in July, if they can get everything sorted in time. (That's the kind of speedy wedding I like!) He says he'll try, but doubts he'll be able to get back for the nuptials: 'I would be miserable not to be there but you will make it up to me some day with lots of kisses. At your wedding you must have a bridegroom but could do without your old Pa!'

Here's the bit I love. Like all fathers, he can't resist giving his daughter advice – and because he's so far away, she's a captive audience.

He writes:

Don't be alarmed or surprised if you quarrel and tell him not to be surprised either! But when you have quarrelled, put aside all pride and vanity and don't hesitate to be the first to make it up. You will probably have fits of rage and roll on the floor and cry. But it soon passes over. Don't overtire yourself. Don't exaggerate in what you do. Use moderation. And go to the dentist to have your teeth looked over, very often. No man can continue to love a wife with bad teeth.

Who were these people? I doubt I'll ever know, but the good sense of it is relevant today. I hope she listened to Pa's counsel.

A few weeks later

AND FINALLY...

You're not going to believe this extraordinary coincidence. Three weeks ago I told you about an old letter I unearthed among papers – one I found years ago, tucked in a piece of second-hand furniture. It was written from Peking by a father (surname illegible) to his daughter, giving her advice on her engagement. He doubted he would make the wedding day. I ended, 'Who were these people? I doubt I'll ever know...'

On that very day, a certain gentleman was on a plane from Sicily to London, with nothing to read. The BA stewardess handed him the *Daily Mail*, which he never usually takes. He read my column carefully and came to the side headline, 'A father's words of wisdom.' And with astonishment realised my subject was his own family.

Now he has written to me. 'My father's name was Daniele Vare. He was Italian and a diplomat by profession ... His letter was to my sister Margherita who was to marry Ranieri di Campello, who later captained the equestrian Italian team at the Olympics.' Yes, all the names are in the letter, even the father's signature now clear. The letter goes on:

I have a spectacular photograph of Margherita's wedding (July 1931) on the steps of St Peter's in Rome. She was extremely beautiful. Next to her the dashing bridegroom in full uniform, shining helmet, a lot of gold braid. My father, who did get there in time, in top hat and tails, my Scottish mother and other ladies in flowing dresses.

Isn't that a glamorous, romantic image?

In turns out that Daniele Vare's diplomatic career ended when Mussolini came to power. He went on to write many books, and one of his claims to fame is a well-known quotation, 'Diplomacy is the art of letting someone have your way.'

His son writes: 'This must be a chance in several million (a) that I should read your article and (b) that now you know all about the letter you found.'

Which will now find its way back from this delighted 'borrower' to its rightful owner.

(And, three weeks later, there arrived in the post a wonderful copy of that 1931 wedding in Rome, before the Second World War. How beautiful they all looked, and how happy in the sunlight.)

You wake up in the morning and lo! Your purse is magically filled with twenty-four hours of the magic tissue of the universe of your life. No one can take it from you. No one receives either more or less than you receive.

Arnold Bennett (English novelist, 1867–1931)

68

WHAT ABOUT ME?

This single, 52-year-old woman lives with her 78-year-old father, takes care of him, and teaches full time. Her 'much-loved' mother died the year before: 'She was very possessive, and if I ever suggested going away on my own, she made a huge fuss over all the terrible things that might happen to me. I managed one trip away – to Italy when I was thirty.' She asks:

'Is this all there is? Recently my solicitor asked me to plan my own funeral because when I die there will literally be no one to do that. I've said I want a stand-up comedian and when the final curtain parts I want to go out to the Doors version of "Light My Fire". I feel that my life has been all about looking after other people and I'd just like someone to look out for me. Is it too much to ask?'

Your final question prompts two responses, one easy and obvious and the other more considered. The easy answer is, 'No, it's not

too much to ask!' Which could be followed by the usual exhorta-
tion to you to look for a new activity so that you can meet people
etc. There is nothing wrong with such advice – and it's very often
useful in jump-starting a life. I've had readers write back with the
good news that joining a dance class or the Ramblers Association did
the trick in (a) cheering them and (b) promising new relationships.

But I am in a quiet, even sombre mood since I heard of the death
(last week) of a truly wonderful young woman aged thirty, after a
four-year struggle against cancer. She was at our wedding in 2007,
her lovely face merry beneath her post-chemo headscarf, and her
spirit 'up' as ever. The world is a more pitiful place without this person who had so much still to give and who believed, right up until
the end, that *any* life is 'worth living'. You know, I sometimes feel
that because so many desperately ill people try so hard to live, and
fail, the rest of us owe it to the beautiful world around us to try to
live 'for' them – with courage, and gusto and hope. Until the end.

Because of that, I want to consider your last question and pose
one of my own: '*Who* is it that you are asking?' You see, many people reach middle age with a sense of disappointment that life hasn't
'delivered'. They haven't found the happiness and love that all of us
are entitled to ... er ... aren't we? Lacking religious faith, they would
not dream of praying for change because that would be pointless.
And so the big 'ask' turns in on itself. We resent nameless destiny
– that dark, empty night sky – yet feel incapable of taking our fate
into our own hands. So I am suggesting that the only person who
can answer that question is you, yourself.

There will be many people tasked with caring for parents (or other
dependents) who will readily (and rightly) join the chorus of 'why
me?' But that question, too, is pointless. I hope you will forgive me

for saying that you must be honest with yourself and see that your beloved, clinging mother was culpable in not allowing you any freedom. It's important that you don't just blame your controlling father for the situation you're in. And here I am going to seize this chance to beg *all* parents of young people to Let Them Go. Leave home to be educated, travel, meet people, do their own thing – not yours.

How to cope with the situation you are in? By knowing that it is temporary. You are doing your duty by your father (and it's important to tell yourself that it matters and that you are a good person) but he will die and then you will be free. That is blunt, I know – but true. Once retired, you can create your own life. You could be bold, leave your backwater and do Voluntary Service Overseas (www.vso. org.uk), taking your skills somewhere in the world where they will be so valued. Oh, the new people! The challenge! Would you have the courage to do that – or something similar? Why not? That song you want at your funeral contains these lines, 'The time to hesitate is through / No time to wallow in the mire? Try now – we can only lose…'

But the day of your funeral is a long way off – God willing.

Don't give up hope. I can only encourage you to believe that it is never too late to light your *own* fire.

The lamps are different –
but the light is the same.

Sufi saying

69

MIXING THE MUSIC

IT DOES SEEM amazing that I've only just unpacked the last boxes, since we moved over a year ago – but that's the way it is. Now my husband and I have decided to do something magnificently 'retro' and put out our respective vinyl record collections, plus the turntable. So he has built shelves that surround the 1964 jukebox in the kitchen, and we love the click and whirr of playing music the old way. Mind you, as I write this I'm listening to music on iTunes, so we have the best of all worlds.

But, it occurs to me that melding two separate music collections is a good test of a marriage. What do we have in common and what do we dislike about the other's taste? As I sorted the LPs into categories and alphabetical order (yes, I am a geek, with the soul of a librarian), I found two copies of Joni Mitchell's 'Blue' and two of Frank Zappa's 'Hot Rats'. Hooray! We also have an overlapping taste in jazz and blues – not to mention Jimi Hendrix and Bob Dylan.

But I had to put his dreaded 'Stranglers' collection on the shelf, plus 'Talking Heads' – which do nothing for me. In turn he smiles at 'Great Heartbreakers' and 'Sixties Love' – not to mention the Everly Brothers and Dionne Warwick. Yet he's impressed that I have a rare 1956 Gene Vincent album – because his much-admired Ian Dury sang of 'Sweet Gene Vincent'. He's also pleased that '50s LPs of Elvis and Bill Haley join the collection – and I point out that's one of the advantages of having an older wife! I bring the Beatles as my dowry while he provides a mighty fine reggae collection. This is all great for dancing to in the kitchen.

What's more, my first precious classical records (many on the budget Supraphon label) are welcomed by him, because he came to such music relatively late. But he will be enthusiastic when I book classical concerts at this year's Bath International Music Festival, even if his taste prefers events that feature jazz or world music. So you see – in mixing the music we have found one secret to a happy marriage: overlapping tastes, but enough differences to keep interest alive.

70

SPRING

WERE YOU AWARE that we have just passed the spring equinox? A vast and awesomely beautiful moon hung in the sky, as if to mark the moment when the tilt of the world's axis means that night and day have approximately equal lengths. From that point in March there are more and more hours of daylight, which is cause for celebration. What's more, at midnight tonight the clocks go forward (remember – 'spring forward but fall back') and so we know that summer is on its way, even if the weather turns cold again. Everyone I know is saying, 'It feels like it's been a very long winter.' And – because of all the pre-Christmas snow – it has indeed.

Now everything in nature is coming alive: seeds germinating, trees sprouting, blossom waiting to burst forth, animals mating … No wonder the pagans worshipped Ēostre, Goddess of Light. Her name is at the root of the word 'Oestrus' which is the time of fertility in mammals: the sexual cycle of being. That universal truth is why spring is celebrated all over the world, as it has been since before recorded time. This is the period of renewal – and it will happen each year, whether or not we are here to see it.

I'm reminding you of this because, though born an urban girl, I feel very much in touch with the natural cycles of the earth – and that's a good thing for all of us. I'm not suggesting you rush out like rutting stags or nesting birds – unless the fancy takes you! On the other hand, animals and birds doing what they gotta do have much to teach us – and NOT about sex! The instinct to renew yourself should go far beyond physical reproduction. Even if you're feeling vaguely down one day, but choose to make a point of staring at a clump of daffodils in a park or window-box, letting that glorious yellow penetrate your soul – then you are creating yourself anew. If you stop and stare at the buds on a tree, really noticing them as if for the first time, then something of their freshness transfers itself to you.

Try it and see.

Live, work, act. Don't sit here and brood and grope among insoluble enigmas.

Henrik Ibsen (Norwegian playwright, poet and theatre director, 1828–1906)

71

YOU GOT A FRIEND

A 55-year-old man is 'dating' a divorced woman (forty-seven), their teenage children all get on very well, and everything seems perfect. Now the lovely lady wants them to move in together, but ... wait ... he is missing 'feelings that I have had in the past – with stomach-lurching moments etc.' He asks, 'Should I be shouting Eureka – I've found the perfect companion and the respect we have for each other will enable us to have a fulfilling life together? Or ... should I go back onto the dating scene, waiting for true love?'

MANY OF THE people who write to this column are enduring real, deep misery, and I'm sure they will read this and cry out, 'What's wrong with you? Is that ALL you have to worry about?' Yet, as I often point out, there isn't really a league table in problems and each person winces at the prick of personal pain, experiencing it uniquely. Actually, I chose your letter because it raises a truly important issue that causes untold misery – and always has. This is the human longing for romantic love. What a pesky and pernicious thing it is – this hankering after the earth moving and the waves crashing on the shore and the bones igniting and breath stopping … and all that jazz.

What is wrong with people that they think perfect happiness is out there, waiting to be felt in the lurch of a stomach? I'm afraid stomach movements always make me think of throwing up. A plague on 'Luurve' I shout. Let's have that stupid Cupid put down.

You must have known I would say this – and express what you know to be the truth. It's as if you are being buffeted by two opposing selves – the sensible one, and the silly, spoilt teenager who wants the upper hand. You have painted a picture of such a good relationship that every lonely reader your age who longs for companionship will want to smack you for being so obtuse. I don't think your issue does 'highlight the choices over fifties need to make while dating'. Believe me, most of them would be eternally grateful to have found what you have – because (to be blunt) they have reached a mature understanding of how rare is the very contentment that you are belittling.

An extraordinary coincidence happened. I studied your letter, which put me in mind of a favourite poem of mine called 'Not Love Perhaps' by a long-neglected poet called A. S. J. Tessimond. Then – believe it or not – in the same postbag I found that a lady called Sylvia, writing with her own problem, had copied out for me that very poem! Amazed, I decided that it must have a message for you – so please Google that poem now. (Though out of print for years, this wonderful poet is reprinted now by Faber Finds.) The poem compares the romantic idea of love 'that many waters cannot quench' with the mutual companionship and support that helps a couple 'walk more firmly through dark narrow places'.

Tessimond celebrates the idea of love as an 'alliance' – though of course, his title ironically questions the very word 'love'. Oh, please let us join in the chorus of 'You got a friend' sung by the great Carole King! Let us be grateful to have found an inn to give us shelter, when the road is dark and empty and the wind blows cold. Let us cherish companionship and learn not to listen to the siren call of this thing called 'true love' – which can wreak such destruction.

Imagine what would happen if this lovely lady were to meet another man next week and experience a *coup de foudre*? Call time on your two-year relationship? I want you to think carefully about how you would feel and value what you have accordingly.

Imagine all that business of dating, all over again. The endless wait for 'true love' – like hunting for a unicorn across all the forests of the world and then wondering on your deathbed why you weren't content with the real, flesh-and-blood creature who showed such devotion.

If I were in a mean mood, I'd tell you that you deserve to have a stomach-lurching episode with a woman who then ditches you, intent on her own search for 'true love'. But I'm not. So I wish you happiness with the one you love. This one.

Sooner or later everyone discovers that perfect happiness is unrealisable, but there are few who pause to consider the antithesis: that perfect unhappiness is equally unattainable.

Primo Levi (1919–87), *If This Is a Man* (1947)

72

A DEATH AT BEACHY HEAD

'Iris' wrote to tell me that, three years earlier, in the spring, her daughter
(forty-four) threw herself off the cliffs at Beachy Head: 'I feel so guilty. I
should have been able to help her. I'm her mother. I knew she suffered from
depression but didn't know how to help.' Grieving Iris lives 300 miles away
and has never been back to the spot since the funeral.

THIS IS SUCH a tragic story and I'm sure I speak for many readers when I admit that it made me bow my head in humility.
Your sorrowful and beautiful letter serves to put into perspective the myriad small irritations of life, and for that I thank you. But
it also reminds me that all our moments of happiness are overshad-
owed by the inevitability of loss, and that is a wake-up call (and
don't we need them?), reminding us all to seize the time while we
can. To live, hope and love.

Somebody who is driven to commit suicide (whether from

quiet despair or anger) blasts apart the lives of family and friends. Underpinning the terrible grief is confusion, guilt and even anger – all merging into the question, 'How could they do this to us?' There is agony in wondering whether, if you could race back to the early years, there might have been conversations that would have increased your understanding and prevented this outcome. Am I right?

You say, 'I'm her mother' in the anguished belief that you of all people should have been able to reach Sally and prevent her death. But how could you? Backed into her cul-de-sac of disappointment, grief and despair (you list some of the reasons) she no longer wanted to live and so refused the therapeutic interventions that just might have helped her. That is no more your responsibility than is the rain which falls from the sky. Mothers will always blame themselves. But all the parental love in the world could not save Sally from the fact that she chose to turn her face towards death – and succeeded on her third attempt. Therefore I wish I could take you by the shoulders, look into your eyes, and whisper, 'This is not your fault.'

You have written because you want me to tell you how to move forward.

Quite rightly you say that talking to a therapist doesn't take the pain away, but it can help you come to terms with issues like guilt. The Child Death Helpline is a freephone service for anyone affected by the loss of a child, at any time and any age. People call because they are still grieving for adult offspring who died years ago. The phones are manned by bereaved parents who have been trained. The number is 0800 282 986 (evenings 7–10 p.m.; Mon–Fri 10 a.m.–1 p.m.; Tue–Wed, 1–4 p.m.) and you might find it useful when you feel you have no one to talk to and don't want to fix that brave face on for the world.

Should you make a pilgrimage to Beachy Head? Yes, I think you should.

First, visualise Sally at a happy moment in her life, perhaps walking her beloved dog (who died before her, adding to her woe) through fields and woods. The sun shining, birds singing. Breathe deeply and focus hard on that image when you feel distraught from grief. I'm not telling you not to be upset, just asking you to see light in the darkness. It is essential that you find some consolation where you possibly can, and the way to do that is to reflect that Sally is now at peace. You could create a special place at home, perhaps a shelf where you stand her photograph and some small things that remind you of her, and light a scented candle. Such little shrines bring calm.

Perhaps you should promise yourself to go back to Beachy Head on the next anniversary of her death (if not before) and throw flowers, telling Sally that you will always love her and that you know she is no longer in pain. Imagine that she can see you and hear the sea birds and the wind and the sea. That she can sense the grass, the flowers, the rocks – and is there within them all, forever. You could even take a letter with you, in which you have poured out all your feelings of guilt, and take a trowel to bury it right there, where it belongs. Pick up a pebble or a fragment of chalk and carry it home to place on the shelf. You will weep – but you will also come to feel that love and beauty are as indestructible as those great white cliffs.

A few weeks later

AND FINALLY...

A month ago I printed a sad letter from 'Iris', consumed with guilt
and grief because her daughter had committed suicide at Beachy
Head. Many of you wrote, moved by her words and my reply. Some
people sent emails and letters for Iris, but I regret to tell you that I
do not have any address, only the northern town where she lives.
Still, your kindness hasn't gone to waste because it adds to what I
know about human nature...

The good news is – Iris herself wrote again after the column
appeared, truly grateful. She intends to follow my advice exactly
as laid out and face up to her sorrow by making a pilgrimage to the
place of her daughter's death: 'I will go in the spring when all the
daffodils are out and take some for her.' She ends, 'I'm crying now
as I write this letter but it's been so good to tell someone how I feel.'

If Iris is reading now I want her to know how moved people were
by her story.

I also want to tell her about two organisations kind readers
reminded me about. The first is The Compassionate Friends, which
(like the Child Death Helpline that I did mention) offers a support
service for bereaved parents. It's been a godsend for certain readers, so I want to remind anyone affected by the death of a child (of
any age) to pick up the phone to one of those helplines when you
need to talk. TCF is 0345 123 2304 and all calls are answered by a
bereaved parent who understands.

Patricia Thomas writes to tell me about her organisation, Survi-
vors of Bereavement by Suicide. She described the comfort people

find through attending a local group and 'over time realising that their overwhelming feelings of guilt are a natural part of their bereavement process'. The website is www.uk-sobs.org.uk and the helpline is 0300 111 5065. I know that for many people it is daunting to pick up the phone to a stranger, but I know for a fact that it can be very comforting.

Thank you to everybody (including Iris) for holding out hands.

And may your lost loved one
Enter into the beauty of eternal tranquillity,
In that place where there is no more sorrow
Or separation or mourning or tears.

John O'Donohue (Irish poet and philosopher, 1956–2008)

I never saw a moor,
I never saw the sea;
Yet know I how the heather looks,
And what a wave must be
I never spoke with God,
Nor visited in heaven;
Yet certain am I of the spot
As if the chart were given.

Emily Dickinson (American poet, 1830–86)

73

THE SPIRITUAL IMPULSE

W E WENT TO see the magnificent, uplifting exhibition 'Treasures of Heaven' at the British Museum – which explores the ancient Christian tradition of preserving holy relics. The bodies of the saints were scattered far and wide in tiny fragments (or so they believed, although there must have been a relics industry...): macabre splinters of bone encased in a costly reliquary or shrine. Even objects supposed to have been touched by a saint were venerated, and pilgrims would make gruelling journeys to worship at their shrines.

Of course, some will find all this rather repellent, but I was entranced – listening to haunting sacred music under the great dome of the old Reading Room and reflecting on the importance of faith throughout the centuries. This week the Prime Minister's ridiculously expensive 'happiness survey' announced certain obvious findings I would have handed to the researchers for free, but they did uncover one fact that may surprise some people. The Office of National Statistics admitted, 'There were considerably more contributions concerning belief or religion, in particular Christianity, than we had expected.'

This comes as no surprise to your columnist. I've observed that you can give people an iPad, a nice car, expensive clothes, or whatever – but those accoutrements cannot begin to answer the question at the heart of life: what it's all *for*. In the harsh, cold light of the medieval world, people knew that. They saw the answer in the walls of their churches and in the cross glittering on the altar.

To bring the glorious exhibition up to date, the museum ends with a film, showing queues for Lenin's tomb, Greek Orthodox worshippers bending to kiss icons, 'pilgrims' wearing Elvis T-shirts at Graceland, Muslims making their sacred journey (Hajj) to Mecca, fans lighting candles at Jim Morrison's grave in Paris, and so on. Remember the aftermath of poor Princess Diana's death? The mountain of flowers and the lighting of countless candles in her memory? In religious and secular life today, people still choose their icons to fulfil a deep need to worship – to look upwards towards something or somebody outside themselves.

And so to poor, doomed Amy Winehouse, who became a tragic relic within her own lifetime. The shrine of flowers and tributes outside her home may seem tacky to you, but to me it's more evidence that – in lives that feel so empty – the spiritual impulse will always find an outlet.

74

PAY ATTENTION

P EOPLE OFTEN ASK me if I ever hear back from people helped
by the column. The answer is yes – and often the happy
responses come from people who haven't actually written to
me with a problem. For example, our 30 July headline asked, 'Am I
silly for wanting my husband to show me some tenderness?' Daphne
(not her real name, of course) had been married for forty years but
was fed up because her husband 'just doesn't see me any more'. She
craved affection and attention.

I wrote this:

*All husbands should buy their wives a bunch of flowers from time
to time. But women, as well as men, need to remember that kind
and appreciative words are bouquets in their own right, and their
effect lasts when real flowers have faded ... In Arthur Miller's
famous phrase from* Death of a Salesman, *'Attention must be
paid.' That is an important maxim all of us would do well to
remember, apropos of our loved ones.*

Now I have received this postcard from a grateful reader:

> I read your column and the situation was mine to a tee. In a mad moment I pushed the article in front of my husband and said, 'You should read this.' He did – and to my astonishment he has taken it on board. What a difference it has made – amazing what a hug can do. We have been married for forty-seven years – so this shows that things can improve. Thank you.

On the subject of marriage, another reader tells me she's been carrying around a cutting from the column for years. Dealing with another marital problem, I quoted the great American writer Edith Wharton – whose words made a big impression on this lovely lady and helped her through her own marriage crisis. This is part of the passage:

> *The years had not been exactly what she had dreamed; but if they had taken away certain illusions they had left richer realities in their stead. She understood now that she had gradually adjusted herself to the new image of her husband as he was, as he would always be. He was not the hero of her dreams, but he was the man she loved, and who had loved her.*

The message is – love the one you're with. And pay attention.

75

AFTER HE'S GONE

Dear Bel,

After twenty-five years in a loving, tactile, wonderful friendship and marriage, my husband (without warning) walked into our kitchen one Saturday evening while I was cooking and said he was leaving. No warning at all, no one else involved ... I know I couldn't have loved him more. I don't feel I will ever get over the rejection or this bewilderment that engulfs me. If it was not for my sons I would take my life. Please give me some hope. I can't go on feeling sick and used. Tell me this pain will ease...

T WILL EASE in the end, but I will not insult you by pretending this will happen soon. Your husband's actions have shattered the very core of a structure you believed to be unassailable – not just the marriage itself, but you yourself, as half of it. Your husband has damaged the identity you took for granted. When one half of a partnership wantonly smashes the whole edifice, he (or she) isn't the one left behind to pick up all the pieces. It's such a cruel, additional injury that – hurt as you are – you're the one forced to sit, dazed, among the fragments.

A few days after your email, I received a similar one from Louise, whose husband also walked out after twenty-five years, telling her he 'loved her but was no longer in love with her'. It was a while ago, but Louise has found it impossible to come to terms with his decision: 'The trouble is, I still love my husband and have always had the hope that he would come back to keep me going.' Her emails ends: 'What is wrong with me? What can I do to put this unbelievably bad chapter of my life behind me?'

We could surmise that both these men went through the proverbial mid-life crisis – and the fact that Louise's husband bought a motorbike is less conclusive proof than his confession to her that 'he wanted to halt the ageing process'. I'm not going to mock that (pathetic though it is) because such a response to middle age is quite normal. 'Halt the ageing process'? You wish, matey! What these men don't realise is that in destroying all they've built up, and abandoning the one who knows them best and loves them most, they can do great harm to themselves too. For a start, they lose the deep-level respect of their grown-up children. Equally important, they have to live with guilt for the rest of their lives – yes, even if the personal outcome is quite happy, in the form of a new love. There will always be a worm in the bud.

But that's enough about the men. What should a wife do in these circumstances? Let's start with Louise's interesting statement, 'the hope that he would come back to keep me going'. Now, of course I understand why a woman needs her partner to sustain and support her, but my gut still rebels at the sheer, needy passivity of that statement. With all my heart and soul I believe that you have to keep *yourself* going, and that nobody else can do that.

A few weeks ago I had an interesting letter from a reader called Jennifer (fifty-nine). She just wanted to tell me about various things that had gone wrong in her life and share her journey towards acceptance. She says; 'I left my lonely marriage when I started a process of self-discovery, over twelve years ago. And all that time I have been becoming my own friend, more and more.'

Her conclusion is rather inspiring and I offer it to you, Gina, and to Louise, as a starting point for thought:

I suppose what I am saying is, it is never too late to find true happiness. And that real happiness can never be found in possessions, or be provided by other people. We have to find a way to make it happen within ourselves, so that we have something truly worthwhile to offer. I would invite your unhappy readers to find a way to (literally) take heart – their own.

I know how hard that is. Of course it seems impossible to listen to such exhortations to love and respect yourself when the man you loved has so smashed your confidence. Nevertheless, this is the starting point. This is the time to find your own voice. After the end of my first marriage, I started to write down poems and extracts and my dreams in a special notebook. Now, in this new life, I find it both wonderful and useful to look back on. One poem that inspired me was 'The Journey' by Mary Oliver (look it up on the internet because I think it may help you). It is about a woman who strides out into her own life, 'determined to do the only thing you could do / determined to save the only life you could save'.

Read it – and be strong. You say you 'are not needed any more'

– but it's not true. Apart from the fact that your sons need you (and so do your friends), the most significant truth of all is this: you need *yourself*. You need to value your 'one precious life' (to quote the Mary Oliver poem I love), no matter what your husband has done to it. Despite what you say, you do not want your husband dead, nor do you wish yourself dead. No. You have too much ahead of you to do – and must start by imagining the fragments glued painstakingly together, by your own hand.

The truth shall make you free
But first it will shatter you.
What was broken can be mended,
What was lost, restored…

Alla Renée Bozarth (American priest and poet, b. 1947)

76

THE GIFT OF POETRY

MORE THAN ONE reader writes that each week they cut out the quotation I chose for the top of this page, to think about. It pleases me so much – because I believe passionately in the power of words to change lives. Reading the poetry of Ted Hughes and Sylvia Plath for the first time in 1967 changed mine forever.

I was just twenty-one, a student of English, about to get married, all life ahead. The two poets introduced me to worlds I had never dreamed of, teaching me truths about human passion and pain, and about our place within the universe, which stay with me now – and which help me write this column. What's more, Ted's books were among the first presents given to me by my first husband, and I treasure them (and his loving inscriptions) still. Life changes, and love may alter as well – but words remain, to give us consolation.

So I was overwhelmed to be one of the guests at the moving ceremony of dedication in Westminster Abbey, when a handsome memorial stone to Ted Hughes was unveiled in Poets' Corner. I sat among poets and other writers, with the spirits of poets all around us, and heard the great Nobel Prize winner Seamus Heaney read Ted Hughes's work and give the address. This to me was the equivalent of a dedicated fan meeting (say) Frank Lampard or Paul McCartney. Yes, we all need our heroes to remind us of what is possible.

There in Poets' Corner his stone sits at the foot of T. S. Eliot's, with Gerard Manley Hopkins just above, and Tennyson, Browning, Auden and the War Poets very near. Seamus Heaney – in his address – said that 'A great poet, a great soul now has his proper place and due.' The beautiful stone, carved by a Devon craftsman, bears these words:

TED HUGHES OM 1930–1998
So we found the end of our journey
So we stood alive in the river of light
Among the creatures of light, creatures of light

Ted Hughes died in 1998 at the age of sixty-eight. A magnificent Poet Laureate, he was (in Heaney's words), 'a guardian spirit of the land and language'. But what many people don't know is that he was also a dedicated educationist, who worked tirelessly to encourage creativity in children, believing that the talent within is 'immeasurable' – and just needs leading out. As he wrote in 1967, '…it is possible … to find the words that will unlock the doors of all those many mansions inside the head … Words that will express something of the deep complexity which makes us the way we are.'

At significant moments in life – and in the great ceremonies of birth, marriage and death – people reach for great words to express their most profound feelings. I am grateful to Ted Hughes (and the rest) for the gift of poetry – and for the life of the imagination that goes on reinventing itself, helping us discover who we are.

…it becomes evident that there is not a place of splendour or a dark corner of the earth that does not deserve if only a passing glance of wonder and pity.

Joseph Conrad (Polish author, 1857–1924)

If we could read the secret history of our enemies,
we would find, in each man's life, sorrow and suffering
enough to disarm all hostility.

Henry W. Longfellow (American poet, 1807–82)

77

DAISY

One December I received a letter from a 22-year-old in despair at the way
her mother treats her – never showing interest in her academic achievements
or any other aspect of her life, and calling her own daughter 'a waste of skin'.
She asks, 'How do I make my mother see that I am worthy of her love and
respect?' and ends, 'I just want her to love me.'

YOU SIGNED YOURSELF 'Deeply depressed' but I have chosen to call you Daisy because I like the name of the resilient,
ordinary little flower – traditionally symbolising innocence
and gentleness – which springs up in the stoniest places. Also, the
daisy's name comes from 'day's eye' – the bright yellow centre like
the sun to which it turns its face. So, I'm offering this identity to
you here as a positive visual image to fix on – preferable to label-
ling yourself as you have done. I entirely understand that you feel
depressed when you think of how your mother has treated you,

wondering what you did to deserve it. But please don't accept this as your identity. Not when you have a wonderful fiancé, a proud father and the hope of a family of your own. Make that truth the sun at the centre of your life.

Telling me that you do love your mother, you ask rhetorically, 'How could I not?' Well, I'll be honest and tell you that (speaking as a devoted mum myself) I can think of dozens of reasons why you shouldn't love this mother-in-name-only. She sounds terrible: a ruthless, cruel, self-centred, lazy, dishonest woman. It goes without saying that she is a damaged person, with issues that prevent her from being able to love, some of which she has passed to you. But please don't expect me to feel sorry for her. We can explain away the worst behaviour by examining causes, but at some stage it's hard to avoid condemnation.

My only concern is with you, and how you can triumph over her legacy. I do wish you had indeed said more in this relatively short email, instead of holding back. Crucially, you don't tell me whether your mother and father are still together. If they are, then I would advise talking to your father to see if he can help to make her see that her behaviour to you is appalling. But I suspect they parted after her affair... Am I right? Whatever the facts, I am convinced that you will not move forward until you stop craving your mother's love. Maybe she does love you in her way (tell yourself that's the case, if it helps) but is incapable of being loving – just as somebody blind from birth cannot learn to see. That is how it is. It will not change. Not now. Pity her if you like, but refuse to be her victim any longer.

So, little Daisy-on-the-stony-ground, what is to be done? This is a good question for a special time of year when some people long to be with their families, but others feel obliged to endure tense gatherings that can even (at their worst) cause real heartache. For many of us, Christmas Day evokes thoughts of those who are no longer there – maybe because of divorce, maybe estrangement, maybe death. The imaginary empty place at the table can make you very sad.

I'm imagining you – a gentle, wistful young woman – looking for the loving mother you know you deserve but did not get. I wish I could become your Fairy Godmother for the day, creating a magic spell to reassure you that you can, indeed, live happily ever after. So – perhaps I will! Instead of yearning for what your mother cannot give, I invite you to open your hands and heart to what is possible. Of course, asking me for 'solutions' is like requesting a miracle. But the Christmas story uppermost in my mind today is a direct invitation to believe (hold your breath) in the miraculous. We think of angels, shepherds and a baby lying in poor surroundings – familiar from so much sacred art throughout centuries. What's more, Mary typifies pure, self-sacrificing motherhood… Oh, there is so much to learn from this story, and you do not have to be a practising Christian (or indeed, a Muslim, since Mary is important in the Koran) to be moved by the message.

Surely one of the lessons for every one of us is how to listen out for the 'good tidings of comfort and joy', even when your own crying threatens to drown them out?

The all-important message for you is contained within the tender promises you have exchanged with the wonderful man who loves you. Remember my mantra: always look forward, never look back – otherwise you will stumble on the road. Even though you didn't learn the art of loving at your mother's knee, you are learning it from others, every day, in a world full of goodhearted people (fairy godmothers and angels in disguise) who will help you – as long as you allow yourself to see them.

That won't happen if you are still (metaphorically) looking for your mother. You won't pick up the good news from the starry sky if you are still hearing her harsh words. Listen to me instead. All good things will await you (piled up like glittering presents under the tree) as long as you realise that the miracle of hope and love is there inside you – your personal private blessing.

('Daisy' contacted me again after this – a wonderful, cheering email. She was very encouraged by my reply and told me I had accidentally chosen for her one of her favourite names.)

78

THE DEATH OF ONE CAT

A S YOU CAN imagine, I receive many emails, some presenting problems, some commenting on issues, and some just
wanting to share thoughts and feelings. Many people write
lovely words about what I have said – and sometimes those I have
advised write back to say thank you. Which always makes my day.

But one of the things we all share is sadness. I have noticed that
advice columns in other newspapers and magazines rarely deal with
bereavement, which is a pity – because there's more to human pain
than love and sex and family squabbles. Yet if you think of Loss as
being central to human life (sad, but true) you see how quickly you
can make the link between the agony of a painful divorce to the loss
of a dying partner or an estranged child. On the other hand, many
people (especially those who have suffered because of the things I
have just mentioned) might believe that if a person expresses real
grief at the loss of a dearly beloved pet, somehow it is trivial.

That's not the case. Read this – which came from a reader called
June, and touched me greatly:

You sometimes comfort people on the loss of a beloved pet dog and I understand that you are a 'dog person'. But I feel that I must tell you of the loss of my beautiful cat. Caspar was seventeen years old and I had him from a kitten. He was an indoor cat and we adored each other. He seemed to know when I was coming home and would wait by the front door or sit on the windowsill to watch. He had kidney failure (although he lived for four years after diagnosis) and yesterday the vet put him to sleep. I am heartbroken – crying as I write this email and my heart like a big stone in my chest. I know eventually the awful pain will ease because I have been through this before, but just wanted to tell you that losing a cat hurts just as much as losing a dog – because I have done both. Thank you for reading.

I know that many readers will understand June's feelings. Such deep feelings for a beloved pet (cat, dog, parrot, no matter) are just another way of enhancing our humanity. The end of the life of one cat has meaning.

Animals are such agreeable friends – they ask no questions, they pass no criticisms.

George Eliot (English novelist, 1819–80)

79

THE SPIRIT CANNOT DIE

Dear Bel,

I am a broken-hearted mother and grandmother. My daughter Sue and her husband David lost their baby Tom at seven weeks, suddenly, the day before Christmas Eve. The whole family's grief has been vast. She was so brave and insisted on a 'normal' Christmas day for her other son Dan aged two. How she gets out of bed each day is a mystery to me. Now although I miss my little grandson like anything, my heart aches most for my own 'little' girl. Remembering the night he died, when she was screaming for him not to go, fills most of my waking day and all hours of my nights. I still see her pleading with my dear departed mum not to let the baby go to her...

I just want to ease her pain somehow. As mothers we are programmed to care and protect our young, no matter what their age, but I CAN'T DO IT. Sue seems to have occasional 'normal' days then feels guilty because of it. All the 'help' charities don't reach our remote area. She has struggled on as best she can, pouring herself into raising money for other bereaved parents.

Can you advise me how to help her? Maybe just writing this will help me a bit as I don't suppose you own a magic wand to take the pain away. Thank you for your time – whoever reads this.

F IRST LET ME assure you that I really do read every single letter; you are not writing to a team in an office but to a real person. What's more, to someone who cried at your short email, since this is an issue very close to my heart – although losing a stillborn son, even at full term (as I did so long ago), cannot be compared with holding and loving a baby for seven whole weeks. As a devoted mother and soon-to-be grandmother I empathise with the anguish and love within your letter.

If I say that the awareness of that love and anguish is all your daughter needs from you, I'm not ducking your question. It's so hard for parents to accept that no specific action can be taken, or words suffice to protect our children from pain. Being there, helping with baby Dan, letting her know that you understand and letting her talk about Tom as much as she wishes … that is what's needed. You are doing your job as a mum and doing it so well. Your letter is proof.

As you say, there is no magic wand – although I am a great believer in the power of prayer (or Will or Visualisation, if you like) and in the fact that time does change the way we experience pain. It isn't that it goes away, it just becomes a part of who we are, like a vein running beneath the surface of the skin. The fact that your daughter has thrown herself into trying to raise money for bereaved parents is (perhaps) the start of that process, but these are very early days. She will experience periods of relative equilibrium, then plunge into despair, but go on doing the best she can for Dan's sake. What else can she do?

You say you live in a remote area, but the Child Death Helpline (childdeathhelpline.org.uk) offers a valuable freephone service for anyone affected by the death of a child – 0800 282 986. The Compassionate Friends (tcf.org.uk) is another brilliant organisation with a similar service – 0345 123 2304. I do urge you to look at the websites (I mention them many times because I really do believe in this kind of service) and pick up the phone when you need to talk. The (trained) bereaved parents who operate both phone lines know what your daughter has only recently discovered – that a child (of any age) who has died goes on being loved forever, and that such love can go on miraculously enlarging the lives of those who feel it. In a sense, that is the deepest 'magic' … that the little spirit cannot die.

The world breaks everyone and afterwards
many are strong at the broken places.

Ernest Hemingway (American author and journalist, 1899–1961)

80

FORGIVENESS

S O OFTEN THE idea of forgiveness runs through my answers
on this page. Surely it's an essential aspect of humanity,
that we are capable of forgiving wrongs by seeking to understand the cause? As the Christian Lord's Prayer says: 'Forgive us
our sins, as we forgive those who sin against us.' I would want
those who are blazing with righteous anger about a perceived
hurt to consider what wrongs they might have done too. I do this
myself and, believe me, it is a very useful piece of advice for war-
ring married couples.

A couple of nights ago I went to a London event organised by a
charity called The Forgiveness Project. Their website (www.thefor-
givenessproject.com) is a repository of extraordinary stories of pain
and reconciliation and I would counsel anybody feeling sorry for
themselves to look at the site and reflect on the accounts of human
pain and courage there. The aim is to 'create a dialogue and promote
understanding of forgiveness and conflict resolution by collecting
personal stories and providing outreach programmes'. They do much

valuable (and fascinating) work in prisons, trying to show inmates that there's a better way to live.

But I want to tell you how humbled I was by hearing Marian Partington speak. She was part of an inspiring panel, yet for me the testimony of this pink-cheeked, grey-haired woman was the most powerful. In front of 700 people she talked, gently but with crystal-clear intelligence, about utter depravity. In so doing she proved that light can, in the end, vanquish the blackest night. In 1973, Marian's younger sister Lucy – a student of literature and art and a budding poet – was abducted from a bus stop by monsters Fred and Rose-mary West, raped, tortured, murdered, dismembered and buried in the Wests' cellar. For twenty-one years her family knew nothing of what had happened to her, and then had to come to terms (how paltry that phrase seems) with the unspeakable horror of what did. How could you live with such knowledge? How to go on?

Rattling back to Bath on a late train, I paused in my reading of Marian's essential, luminous, transforming book, *If You Sit Very Still*, to stare out at the darkness. In my mind I still heard her voice speaking from the platform that night: 'To nurture a flame of hatred would be deeply corrupting of my own humanity.'

And rain slashed the window, like tears.

81

RELIGION OR FREEDOM?

This young woman is sixteen and trapped in a religion she will not name.
She wants to leave it but fears hurting her family and being disowned by
them. Elsewhere, she says, she could be killed for her beliefs. If she tells
her parents of her inner turmoil 'my chances of getting good GCSEs and A
levels will be ruined ... but if I don't have the courage to tell my family I'll be
trapped in a religion, being someone I don't want to be. And even the fact
that I'm a female makes it worse as I have noticed that men in this culture are
treated better and thought of as more important.'

With no one to turn to she wants to know what I would do.

THIS IS A very interesting letter and I'm touched you felt you
could write. I can hazard a guess at your religion, but won't
risk inventing an inappropriate pseudonym. Let me say immediately that I wouldn't dream of dismissing you in patronising words

like 'only a phase'. At sixteen you are perfectly capable of forming your own opinions on this, and many other issues.

I ask you to realise that honest doubt is not only a part of the human condition, it's a noble state of mind. Roads towards faith or doubt fascinate me, which is why I made five interview series for Radio 4 called *Devout Sceptics* about the subject. The programmes were very much liked by the audience because there are so many people – whether Christian, Muslim, Hindu or Jewish – who feel as you do and therefore enjoyed hearing others wrestle with their sense of the spiritual and their rejection of one god.

Nowadays I call myself a 'questing agnostic', yet religion (and the church) is still important to me. Perhaps one day you will feel the same, able to take charge of your own views (as you've started to do) while not rejecting out of hand the culture of your upbringing. No one can control your private doubt, since you have reason on your side. For it's sadly true that religious observance need have no effect on moral behaviour while the atheist can be morally upright, with no faith other than a sense of duty towards humankind.

You say you have no one to talk to – but does your school have a counsellor or teacher in charge of student welfare? I'd be happier to know that there was an understanding adult nearby you could turn to, so please look into this. Concerning your family, I feel it's too early for you to tell them your feelings; far more important for you to leave school with good grades than to cause a massive family upset. I realise it is very hard for you to go through the motions of following your religion, yet why not be philosophical about this, as a temporary measure, while cultivating your inner life? Three years will pass very quickly, and then (hopefully) you will be able to leave for higher education. Perhaps you could get hold of a book about all religions (Dorling Kindersley has an accessible Eyewitness Companion), which you can be seen to be reading, to show your parents your intellectual curiosity. If they question this, it could be for school. In your place, I would keep quiet, remain strong, and cultivate the most important faith of all – the belief in your own spirit.

Let the beauty we love be what we do;
There are hundreds of ways to kneel and kiss the ground.

Rumi (Persian poet and mystic, 1207–73)

82

DOES A DOOR OPEN?

Three years ago this 75-year-old man's wife suddenly walked out of their 'lovely modern bungalow' and ended the marriage. He thought they were happy: 'She was my world.' Four months later he found she'd moved in with someone else. 'I have lost everything that meant so much to me and I do not understand. Everybody keeps telling me that when one door closes another opens. How long must I keep waiting?'

YOU HAVE WRITTEN a heart-breaking letter that I have no idea how to answer. That's why I've chosen to print it – to show the limits of what someone like me can say. Readers often tell me they read the letters then imagine how they'd reply, and only then read my own attempt at wise advice. How would they answer you – those kindly readers who care about the problems of others?

It would be insulting to come up with glib formulaic phrases. You have lost so much and are still reeling from the shock of having your life turned upside down – of discovering that the woman you loved was capable of such deceit and that the life you loved was not valued by her. Something was wrong – but you didn't know it. Maybe you could have noticed more, talked more … but who am I to guess? All I can say is that I am very sorry – and then bow my head before the enormity of your final question. Because – truthfully – I have no answer for the problem of great pain like yours.

Waiting? I suppose it's true to say that you will wait until the day comes when you don't feel the loss quite so savagely. Perhaps someone or something will suddenly delight you, and you will feel the shade miraculously lift. That is how it can happen – quite unexpectedly, and I wish it for you with all my heart. As I become older I realise, with humility, that existence (for so many people) is a matter of sheer endurance. The true human grandeur lies in the defiance which goes on keeping us alive.

Now let me introduce you to Will – a man of your generation who is also suffering a bereavement (Yes, Ricky, that is essentially the nature of your loss) and wrote an anguished letter that moved me greatly. Will is eighty-three and his beloved wife died in April, aged ninety-two, after fifty-two years of marriage. He gives lots of detail about her illnesses, as well as their companionable life. Then he writes:

I was always with her. Now I feel so lonely, I wander round the house, do silly things like visiting supermarkets to buy things I don't need, but I'm all alone … I still can't believe she has died, all this seems so unreal. Forgive me for writing, Bel, but I feel I'll go mad unless I tell somebody. There is nothing left any more and sometimes I wish I could join her.

You might think that Will's condition is easier than yours, because he was not betrayed. Such value judgements are impossible. What you share is a need to take the next – very difficult – step. That's why my urge to give practical advice is strong. If each of you two men picked up the phone in an effort to help yourselves to take a single pace forward ... Well, surely that would be better than drowning in bewilderment as well as tears? Since you both wrote proper letters I know where you live – and so would urge Will to get in touch with his local Age Concern Support Service and also Cruse Bereavement Care.

To you, Ricky, I suggest a phone call to an organisation called Evergreen Care Trust to see what they do and whether you can help and/or be helped. And did you know that there is a University of the Third Age in your town? So much is going on! To find out more go to Trinity Methodist Church on Barn Hill on the first Monday of every month (except bank holidays) for coffee and a meet and greet. You never know what might come of it.

Does a door always open when one closes? Well, that's too simplistic. But I do believe that no door will swing open for you if you remain seated, seething or weeping, with your back to it. So force yourself to rise, turn round, and grasp the handle. You have to accept what has happened in order to defy it. Don't wait any longer – but act.

...and then the day came when the risk to remain tight in a bud
was more painful than the risk it took to blossom.

Anaïs Nin (Cuban–American author, 1903–77)

83

ROUND AND ROUND

D O YOU REMEMBER that news story that cheered this gloomy summer – about the Salford grandfather who withdrew £1,000, tripped over and watched his precious cash blow away? Poor Barry Eastwood was in despair – when he was saved by the honesty of passers-by, all ages, all races, who chased the money and returned it all, except a single £20. It's a good one to remember, when you feel pessimistic and believe everybody's in it for themselves.

I remembered that when my son had a similar experience recently. But first, let's go back four years, to when he was living in west London. At the cash point in Notting Hill a young couple were drawing out money. Dan was standing behind them, chatting on his phone. When they strode away, he ended his call, moved forward – and saw they'd left their cash behind. He grabbed the wad, saw there was a lot of cash there, did a rough count… Seeing no sign of them on the main road, he sprinted in the direction they'd taken, turned down a side street and saw them ahead. You can imagine their shock and gratitude when he handed over the £250.

Fast forward to this summer, and Dan has taken his very rare 1964 VW ice-cream van to a classy craft fair in Devon. He and his wife have a business, The Splitscreen Ice Cream Company, selling gourmet ice cream from their elegant, cultish vehicle, at festivals, weddings, trade fairs and other events. It's been in magazine photoshoots too but this year the terrible weather has made business tough. On this particular day, he is preoccupied because he is coping alone (wife at home with the new baby) and the forecast is dire. To cut to the chase – he drives off to park his trailer, leaving on the ground the black bin bag containing a £500 float. It's not until an hour later that he realises. Panic. He's worked very hard for that money. Heart thumping, he rushes to the main gate, praying somebody might have handed it in. The organisers shake their heads. At that very moment, two women arrive with the bag and Dan falls on his knees before them to say thank you.

As they say – what goes round comes round.

84

LARKIN ABOUT

O N THURSDAY NIGHT I raised a glass to that grumpy old genius Philip Larkin – who remains one of this country's greatest poets. It would have been his ninetieth birthday – although sadly he reached only sixty-three. There's a fine statue of him in Hull station, a flourishing Larkin Society and a small, perfect legacy of work. You could open Larkin's collected poems at any page, on any day, and find something to echo your deepest moods, light as well as dark.

But what a cliché his most famous poem has become. I don't mean the one where he says that, 'Sexual intercourse began / In nineteen sixty three / (Which was rather late for me)' – although I recommend its light-hearted dryness. No – it's Larkin's harsh, disillusioned attack on the family that people love, and commit to memory. 'This Be The Verse' begins with the famous line, 'They fuck you up, your mum and dad' and ends, bleakly, with 'And don't have any kids yourself.' (If you don't know it you can find it on the internet, but I do recommend the books.)

Well, we all know the bad news about families, and (believe me)
I get enough sad and bitter letters to please the most sardonic side
of Larkin's shade. But I am choosing to celebrate the great man's
birthday by sticking my tongue out to mock his cynicism. So here
is my own take on 'This Be The Verse' – dedicated to all those who
cherish a less jaundiced view of family life.

> They build you up, your mum and dad
> It's what they're there for, so they do;
> They hand on foibles that they have,
> But add some virtues, just for you.
> And they were built up, in their turn,
> By folk in old style coats and gloves,
> Who, though they might have seemed too stern,
> Still quietly handed on their love.
> You may inherit small, sad wrongs.
> Which deepen like a coastal shelf,
> But there's a chance to sing new songs,
> So try – by having kids yourself!

85

THREE YEARS LATER...

Dear Bel,

Every week I read your column and for the last three years I've taken great comfort in knowing I'm not alone in suffering the heart-destroying pain of discovering that my husband of twenty-nine years was betraying me with a very young family friend. The very fact that I could read about other people out there who (like you, in your book) were getting on with their daily lives and turning a brave and smiling face to the world gave me the strength to carry on.

Three years after that discovery and eighteen months from when I eventually took legal advice, I'd hoped that I'd feel much better. I do pretend I'm feeling great so my family and friends don't worry. But at times I find the pain unbearable, I have two adult children living with me who are still suffering too. To hear my daughter say, 'I wish a bus would drive into our house and kill the three of us so that we would be put out of our misery' is so agonising. I don't show them how awful I feel and try to remain upbeat.

They are intelligent, lovely young people on the brink of exciting fulfilling careers and relationships, yet even that doesn't obliterate the misery they still feel because of their father's actions. Now, at fifty-eight, I am looking for more work and struggling to keep my home. I search desperately for a light at the end of this deep, dark tunnel and long to feel happy again. Just being able to write this down is helpful.

TELLING ME THAT reading this column gave you 'the strength to carry on' is like presenting me with a beautiful bouquet… The process you describe is of inestimable importance; we share each other's stories with honesty and generosity in order to help make sense of the world. Sometimes in a dark hour, something read or perhaps heard on the radio can act like a small electric shock, connecting you to the pain of another and helping you (even in a tiny way) to cope with your own. In desperation we cry, 'Why *me?*' to the silent sky. Then one day the pitiful – or brave – sound of another human soul can make us wonder, 'Why *not* me?'

That process of give and take is why I suggest that it's time for you to be utterly honest with the two offspring who are still sharing your life. If you insist on being falsely bright and brave, you are allowing them to continue behaving like hurt, disappointed children rather than adults. When your daughter expressed that wish for a collective family death she was indulging in self-pity at the expense of her own mother, who is miserable and struggling to keep a roof over her head. If she expresses such negative thoughts again, it's time for you to rebuke her briskly: 'None of us want to die, thank you very much, just because yet another man followed his stupid loins!'

Yes, her father let her down and hurt them both, but things do change – if we let them. I'm afraid it's about moving on, coming to terms, getting over it– and other clichés. Truisms are true! Soon (as you say) those two will go on to live their own lives. But you are the one who'll go on bearing the brunt of the grief. You are the one who will have to cope when they move on to their 'exciting, fulfilling careers and relationships'. So you need to sit down with them and be honest about what you feel. As long as they allow their father's actions to go on making them suffer, then he is the victor – and as long as they give him that power, they are making things harder for their mother.

Reassure them that you do understand the extent of their loss. It's one of the great mistakes society makes to assume that separation and divorce hit young children harder than grown ones. Adult children feel furious and humiliated when their father goes off in search of lost youth with a younger woman. It can affect their self-image, as well as destroying the pedestal on which they perhaps placed him. And after all, they've had longer than young children in which to build fantasies about what it will be like to bring home a serious love to meet Mum and Dad. Believe me, I understand all that and sympathise with what they've endured. But still, enough is enough. It's time for them to support you instead of making you feel worse.

I'm wondering if being open and firm with them at last might prove helpful to you too. With luck, speaking your mind and talking through how you can all move forward will enable you to see more clearly too. I can't promise light at the end of the tunnel yet, just a match to light the way. When you discovered that your husband was unfaithful (and with a young family friend, to add insult to injury), life, as you had known it, ended. Eighteen months ago you finally realised he was gone for good, and took legal advice. But you see, it's all still very fresh. There's no quick-fix sticking plaster for such wounds. Had your husband died three years ago you'd still be going through the drawn-out process of grieving. Yet, in a crucial way, he *did* die. The man you'd loved and trusted for twenty-nine years was no more.

You said that writing the email to me was helpful. Building on that thought, I suggest you ask your children each to write a letter to their father, letting him know exactly what they felt when he left and what they think of him now. Ask them to do this for your sake – and you do the same. Take time over it. Tell him why you loved him, put down what was best about your life together (it will make you weep but no matter) and then berate him for what he did and its long-term effects. Hold nothing back. The three of you will then discuss what to do with the sealed letters – which you won't be posting. A ceremonial burning is the best option, so see if you can make that work. Fire purifies – and when the smoke drifts upwards into the atmosphere, with the three of you watching it, you will experience a mysterious cleansing. You have reached the end of one phase in your life, Annie, and the next one is just around the corner. The three of you should raise a glass to that future.

The world asks of us
Only the strength we have and we give it.
Then it asks more, and we give it.

Jane Hirshfield (American poet, b. 1953)

86

BURY BULBS

IT'S THAT TIME of the year again when merchandising rules and we seem to be heading in the same direction as America, where Hallowe'en is big business. There, every local restaurant is festooned with fake cobwebs for weeks. Here, too, pester-power turns small children into ghouls, but anxious parents have to explain that knocking on doors screaming 'Trick or treat?' may not be such a good idea. There are plenty of real ghouls out there.

It always makes me smile when people say 'Happy Hallowe'en' – because it's such a contradiction in terms. Hallowe'en (or, properly – All Hallows' Eve) is about death, mourning, darkness and remembrance – and that's why the 'festival' speaks to our innermost selves, even if we don't realise it. You may close the curtains on the darkness, but … *sshhhh* … it is already inside and cannot be escaped. The name of the great unknown is Mortality and it taps eerily on the window of the soul.

Even in a secular age the subconscious mind tunes into the spiritual at this time of year. Children dressed as witches and skeletons and parents laboriously carving out pumpkin lanterns are connecting to our ancestors and enacting the deeper meaning of 31 October.

It's not hard to see how the idea of the dying of the light prompts thoughts of death. The Celts believed that on 31 October the border between our world and the 'other' world is especially thin. At the time when plants are dying, they believed that revered ancestors reach back through the veil that separates them from the living.

Across cultures, we are similar under the skin – having to find ways of making sense of the world and our place in it. At the close of autumn, drifts of leaves are a reminder of the great cycles of death and renewal. Leaves fall – and so do we. There is nothing to be done about either phenomenon. We may try to keep the darkness at bay with all the gewgaws of modern living, but no plasma screen will protect you from painful truths that the Mexican laughs at on the Day of the Dead.

So, my advice now is – bury bulbs in the good earth.

87

MR MOLE

I T'S A GOOD idea to be ready to see small life lessons in the most unexpected quarters. The other morning a tiny drama played out by our own back door.

We found a mole in the open porch. Three wide steps lead down to the space for recycling and wellies. He must have scurried over the first step in the darkness, then – desperately seeking a way back to grass and soil – tumbled down the other two. Now he was running around, stopping every now and then to scrabble frantically at the concrete with those sharp little claws. If I were writing one of my children's stories, I'd put words in Mr Mole's mind: 'I must tunnel, dig, dig, dig – back to where the fat worms live.' He turned and turned about in his little black velvety coat, wide pink 'hands' outstretched – stranded.

Blindly, he scratched and scraped to no avail, getting more frantic and emitting tiny, high hisses of fury and fear. He didn't know that the humans were watching. Then one bent down and offered the 'tunnel' of a boot, as refuge. In he went, to disappear into the musty darkness of the toe. Then he was carried over to the field and tipped to safety in the grass.

I smiled to think of his relief. Then I couldn't help likening his plight to the human one – when we miss the path, take the wrong turning, tumble down unexpected steps or box ourselves into a cul-de-sac. Sometimes we become angry, sometimes afraid. Or we panic blindly and make the situation so much worse, twisting until we're dizzy and have lost all sense of direction. That's the point at which many people write a letter to me – and often remark that the very act of writing has clarified matters. Just as Mr Mole couldn't possibly know he was watched by kind souls, so some people never realise that there is assistance out there, if they would only seek. So don't wear yourself out trying to tunnel through concrete. Be ready to find a little help in the most unexpected quarters.

Take refuge in your senses; open up to all the small miracles you rushed through.

John O'Donohue (Irish poet and philosopher, 1956–2008)

88

A MESSAGE OF HOPE

P EOPLE OFTEN ASK if I ever hear back from people whose
letters have appeared. 'Sometimes' is the answer – but I just
received a wonderful update from a 26-year-old who begins:
'You might not remember me but I wrote to you four years ago…'

Actually, I did remember, because she described her 'bright hair,
tattoos and piercings' and that was unforgettable. I called her Imogen
and published her letter along with the headline, 'I'm sad, lonely, and
fear I will self-harm again.' Imogen had many problems, including
depression, an eating disorder and coming to terms with the self-
loathing caused by date-rape. She'd dropped out of university and
felt nothing but despair.

I gave advice on many different levels, and that was that. Now
I'm utterly delighted to hear this:

You encouraged me to seek counselling and move back to where my friends
and family were. Well, I did all that, and everything else you said … I don't
want to write an essay but I just wanted to check back in with you and tell

you that I'm doing great. I still have some bad days with the weight issues but I'm healthy, eating well. I'm still with my boyfriend and we now live together in a lovely house in my home town. I haven't had the urge to self-harm in over three years and I am at university again. And guess what? I found my calling, thanks to you! I am just about to finish the first term of my first year as a student studying BA (Hons) Counselling and Psychotherapy. I love it. I'm not saying I'm over everything, I still have nightmares about what happened when I was seventeen but it doesn't control me any more and I have a loving, supportive home and family. So this is just a Thank You. It was the first steps, encouraged by your kind words, that helped me get here and I am forever grateful.

Well, so am I grateful. I can't gift-wrap Imogen's message and put it under our Christmas tree, but it's a present I want to share with you all – as a message of peace, goodwill and (above all) hope.

As to me I know nothing else but miracles,
Whether I walk in the streets of Manhattan…
Or stand under trees in the woods…
To me every hour of light and dark is a miracle…

Walt Whitman (American poet, 1819–92)

89

THE WOLF OF WORRY

This reader was bedevilled by 'anxiety, pessimism and a feeling that I won't cope with what life may bring'. Everything worries her, from the future of the NHS to her marriage: 'I feel so vulnerable. What messages of joy are there? Where lies happiness? I feel so far from being the optimistic woman I was. I love your quotations and think you'll like this:

A grandfather said to his grandson, "My son, there is a battle between two wolves inside each one of us. One is evil: anger, fear, jealousy, greed, resentment, anxiety, lies and ego. The other is good: joy, peace, love, hope, humility, kindness, empathy and trust." The boy asked, "Grandfather, which wolf wins? Quietly, the old man replied, "The one you feed."'

Finally, she adds, 'How can I believe in my own ability to enjoy life?'

T HE DAY I read your letter is known as Blue Monday – alleg-
edly the most depressing day of the year. There is no scientific
basis to that theory, but no matter – late January is a test-
ing time, with festivities over and summer far away. But isn't it the
same in February and chilly March? April and May offer promises
they often break, while June, July and August are so often rainy disappointments. Do you see what I mean? There is always a reason
to feel 'down' – if you allow it. At such moments I tend to turn to
writers for spiritual uplift – Primo Levi, for example. In 1943, the
25-year-old chemist was deported to Auschwitz. His experiences are
set down in a remarkable set of books (start with *If This Is a Man*,
also called *Survival in Auschwitz*), which should be required reading
for all those inclined to indulge in the notion of a Blue Monday or
to wear out the spirit worrying about things that have not happened.

This may seem an odd way to begin a 'message of optimism' –
when you are already afflicted by an awareness of pain. But sometimes
you need to confront real darkness before you can see the light. In
truth, few can open a daily newspaper or listen to broadcast news
without feeling temporarily blighted by the world we live in. Surely
that is normal, at least in anybody with a brain and an imagination?
What isn't 'normal' is to let feelings of doom have such a negative
effect on your life. So I'm glad you've consulted your doctor and urge
you to take any measures to restore balance. Since so much in your
life is good, you perhaps need to break it down a little, to discover
the origin of the worm in the bud.

The only thing to do, when convulsed with horror at the evil
people do, is to remember that it is always balanced by the good. Yes

– always. Once again, the word 'balance' is key. Somebody suggested to me that three-pronged connectivity is the source of happiness. You have to connect with yourself, by taking care and making time for what you love. Connect with others, by working on meaningful relationships. And connect with the larger world or society, by doing things, either through work or otherwise, that bring satisfaction. If one or other of those three levels is out of balance – or disconnected – it is very easy to topple into a black hole of despair.

With all that in mind, it sounds to me as if you might be in the wrong job. Certainly being so tired and stressed by your work will have a detrimental effect on everything else you experience. Think about that and consider what you can do to make this aspect of your life better. Please do not weigh down your new relationship with worries about divorce not endured or children as yet unborn! How does love thrive? By being added to daily. And while thinking about adding to the sum total of who you are, why not consider whether you can channel all your concerns in a useful way, perhaps by volunteering?

Here are two nuggets of wisdom for you from wonderful writers I know personally, each of whom has experienced great sorrow, enough to test the strongest soul. One offers what I might call the Primo Levi corrective:

It sometimes really does help to make a list of things you are NOT. Not in prison, not on death row, not with news of your terminal illness, not penniless, not sleeping on the street, not...
The list is endless but I find imagining being in one of these situations and then knowing I am not, after all, does put things into perspective.

And the other:

When we are in a low state we need techniques: practical habits, even tiny ones, to work up from. Start each day asking for the strength to accept what it brings; end each day writing down three things about it you're grateful for. Even if it's your breath, your bed and the knowledge that things change. And, trite though it can seem to people who don't need it, the famous Serenity Prayer.

I do like your story about the grandfather and the wolves – very much. So feed that good wolf. Take him on a walk into the garden today, to see the wonder of fresh green shoots pushing up through frozen soil, as they always do. Let their unassailable promise of spring push into your heart too.

90

ICE AGE

I N 1963, I left England for the very first time to travel all the way to Paris, where all I wanted to do was visit art galleries. Yes, the shops were exciting, but instinctively the seventeen-year-old knew that art could help her understand the world. Fifty years later, I haven't changed – which is either a cause for celebration or worry, depending on how much you value the need for progress!

So here I am, still having marvellous encounters with great art, which go on teaching me about the human spirit – and that includes (for better, for worse) most of the things that appear on these pages, week after week. Love, power, restlessness, fear, envy, aspiration, dreams… All such emotions are timeless. No wonder my latest illumination came within the great portals of the British Museum, where I caught up with the exhibition, Ice Age Art. It was intensely moving to gaze at small works of art created as far back as 40,000 years ago and to feel such an intense rush of affection and respect for our ancestors.

Because all human life was there. In unbelievably tough conditions they sat around fires in their caves, telling stories, painting animals and people on the walls, playing flute-like instruments and carving chunks of stone or the tusks of mammoths to create representations of what mattered most to them in that long-ago world. Why would do you do that – putting in so much effort to carve a man with the head of a lion, or a sweetly elegant horse, or a pretty girl with waving hair, or a bird in flight? Why would you scratch away to make beads or to decorate a baton that just helped throw spears? Above all, why want to create so many little, plump, pregnant women?

Because making art shouts to the darkest sky that there is more to humankind than simply staying alive. The objects in this enthralling exhibition connect the men and women who made them to you and me. They possessed little but had a sense of purpose and an imagination that could transform the everyday. And we do too.

A very small degree of hope is sufficient to cause the birth of love.

Stendhal (French writer, 1783–1842)

91

LIVE THE LIFE

ABOUT FIFTEEN YEARS ago, I wandered into a small gallery in California selling 'alternative' artworks. I still have the one I bought: watercolour rainbow abstracts around words by the nineteenth-century American author Henry David Thoreau: 'Live the life you've imagined.'

At the time, I thought those words profound. Living in a farmhouse, surrounded by family, writing my children's books, I often dreamed of escape. I supposed I chafed at marriage, at what I had. It wasn't that I was unhappy; I just fantasised about long motorbike journeys, about hanging out in New York as I did in my late twenties, about the Australian outback at sundown when the clink of icy beer is the purest music, about handsome strangers whispering sweet nothings in my ear. The life 'imagined' seemed preferable to reality: middle-aged woman marooned on a windy hill in chilly England.

The quote actually begins, 'Go confidently in the direction of your dreams.' I liked that too. The trouble is … reality and 'talent' television shows have somewhat tarnished the idea of 'living the dream'.

Overconfident delusions sadly deceive the talentless. What's more, it sometimes seems that too many people (especially the young) yearn hopelessly to live the life they've imagined – to the extent that, if they can't morph easily into a pop singer or an overpaid premier league footballer, life isn't worth living at all. Gloomily I gaze at pictures of the latest lottery winner spraying champagne (such a waste of the good stuff!) and think, 'Yes, and your dream is what? Three hideously expensive cars and unhappiness?'

I confess I've changed my mind and these days think of that popular Thoreau quote as glib – a catchpenny phrase containing as much real wisdom as the spouting of a New Age 'guru'. I took it down from my wall, thinking, 'How's about living the life you actually have – and making it as good as possible? How's about going confidently "in the direction" of what you can do to make things realistically better?' I'm not saying we shouldn't have aspirations. But surely hopes and dreams start in the love you have for your one precious life? Or maybe I have decided that being a contented middle-aged wife in a different farmhouse in chilly England is what I always wanted, after all.

Happy the man, and happy he alone,
He who can call today his own:
He who, secure within, can say,
Tomorrow do thy worst for I have lived today.

John Dryden (English poet, 1631–1700)

92

WORKING MUM

This agonised email came from a mother racked with guilt for working full time, because they needed the money and she was the main breadwinner. This is a common problem. She writes: 'I just can't get over the feeling that working full time makes me a bad mother. I often cry because I hate the fact that the staff at the nursery have spent the day playing with him, teaching him, doing the things that I WANT to do with him, but can't because I work. Please can you offer me some advice?'

A s I PUT an imaginary arm around you, my first piece of advice is heartfelt. Are you listening carefully? OK. You are obviously a really wonderful mother and because of that you must stop worrying, for the sake of your whole family. If you weren't good and loving you would not have written to me in this way – because love, care and responsible intelligence shine through every word of your email.

You speak of guilt so allow me to share my own. I have to assume you read my article in which I reported on a conference held by the charity What About the Children? and asked:

When will policymakers talk about mothering? Or acknowledge that the uniquely close relationship between a mother and her baby is vital? Getting mothers back to work has been an obsession of politicians (especially Labour) for decades. I consider myself a feminist and understand the urge (as well as the economic need) to work. But I believe we also need to ask a truly radical question: whether 'outsourcing' mothering is the best way to create a healthy society.

There was much more in that vein. Sometimes journalists write articles in good faith, but also with the awareness that their words may have an effect they're not entirely happy with. I wrote that article because I believe this society is careless about the emotional welfare of children. The argument that young babies need constant, high-quality, loving care must be heard and female commentators should acknowledge that it is *not* all about the mothers' wants or needs. But then comes your letter – making me sorry that my words may have exacerbated your guilt. There's no answer for either of us, is there? The situations we're dealing with are complicated and most of us have to accept muddle and compromise as we struggle to be honest and do what is right.

You didn't want me to disclose the nature of your job, but I know it matters. Your partner is less fulfilled, and I suppose in the ideal world he'd have become the principal carer for your son (many men find this a good option) or a grandmother would have obliged, in the traditional way. On the other hand, the world is not ideal, you need that second wage and grandmothers have their own lives to lead. So what is to be done? Exactly what you are doing. Your son isn't upset; he loves the nursery and he will certainly be gaining excellent social skills. You are devoted and attentive parents all the rest of the time. In other words, you are 'good enough'. As good as you possibly can be. My advice is to embrace that idea – letting it soothe your mind and relax your shoulders and drive your guilt away on wafts of sweet aromatherapy. Good enough. As best as can be. Fine. So 'everything's gonna be all right' as Bob Marley sang.

My children are adults now, with kids of their own, and their memories of childhood are warmly gratifying. They remember all the good bits about their mum – not what a bad-tempered, impatient, tired and stressed baggage I could be. That's how it works in loving families, you know. So here's what I think you should do. Ask Nana to babysit very soon, and arrange to meet two close friends for a movie and a pizza. Crack open the wine, laugh, chat about non-baby things, enjoy yourself. It will do you and your partner so much good. And you deserve that.

*May the door of this home be wide enough
To receive all who hunger for love…
May the door of this house be narrow enough
To shut out pettiness and pride, envy and enmity…*

The Siddur of Shir Chadash (Hebrew prayer book)

93

HATRED AND CONSOLATION

REGULAR READERS KNOW I always try to be honest. Sometimes you tell me you think you know me, think of me as a friend. Therefore I'm confessing that your columnist is feeling very low indeed. Dispirited. It began when Lady Thatcher died … then became worse and worse. Sometimes I just want to stop reading newspapers and switch off the computer forever.

When George Osborne shed a tear at Lady Thatcher's funeral, he had no idea that he was caught on camera. Poor man. He might have been thinking of a loved one, been touched by the Bishop of London's story of the small boy, been stirred by the great music and the extraordinary ceremony … there are many reasons to cry at any funeral. They touch feelings deep within us.

Immediately the Chancellor was jeered at, excoriated, scorned and pilloried, his sincerity doubted, his private tear linked to his public office and all that he has done to 'oppress the people of Britain'. People even suggested he took an onion with him to St Paul's so that he could fake tears. The events of the last ten days have reminded me of the terrifying degree to which cynicism and hate have taken over our society. It is the kind of ideological viciousness that would roll you and I along in a bloody tumbrel towards the killing fields.

I know we should laugh off the loonies spraying champagne at the death of Mrs Thatcher, like rich F1 drivers. But I'm finding it hard to shrug or laugh. I'm repelled by those with whom I'd have once found some common cause and depressed by the ignorant cruelty unleashed daily. How fascinating that the godless ones invoked medieval ideas of hell for Lady Thatcher – who is now at peace.

The philosopher Jean-Paul Sartre wrote, 'Hell is other people.' Yes, it is we who are left to struggle in this hell of widespread hatred, swirling on the web and social networks. We who are poisoned by the miasma of negativity and a widespread lack of empathy that poisons the very air we breathe. And that spits on a man shedding a tear at a funeral.

One week later

AND FINALLY...

In a wise bestseller, *The Secret of Happy Parents*, Steve Biddulph throws light on the pessimistic gloom that I confessed to you last week. Biddulph writes:

We are intended to be truth seekers, life-bringers, but this image of ourselves has all but been lost in modern life. Every night the TV 'news' presents to us, in vivid detail, the tiny proportion of places where the human race is going wrong. Imagine if the TV news were governed by a sense of proportion: Here is the news.

Six billion people today got fed, co-operated with each other, and were really nice to their children. A few slipped up, but nothing worth mentioning. And now here's the weather…

It's a point worth repeating. And it so happens that many of the millions who lead uneventful but magnificent lives read this newspaper! I know it because they write to me – not just with problems, but with consoling stories, humour, bravery and wisdom. And never more so than after last week's 'And Finally' column. I have been totally overwhelmed by the beauty and optimism of your extraordinary response to my sadness and disillusion.

Judith Jones says: 'People are good and we will get better together.' Jill Mazillus reassures me: '…remember that just as you are here for us, so we are here for you'. Patricia Smith is eloquent:

Amid all this apparent confusion it is important to remember that hope exists. Everyone who wants to make a difference and restore some semblance of decency and empathy and understanding has the ability to make that difference. Every single day people face challenges of faith and self. It is easy to feel cast adrift and isolated. If you believe nothing else believe in yourself and your ability to make a difference in other peoples' lives. Remember the countless words of hope and comfort and inspiration you bring others. Banish the negative words and images. Take a little time out to reflect on the extraordinary gifts in your life. Nurture yourself and feed your soul.

There were so many more like that – each letter a jewel. Words like those are a glorious reminder of the extraordinary power of the human spirit. So thank you for restoring my faith.

May you travel in an awakened way
Gathered wisely into your inner ground;
That you may not waste the invitations
Which wait along the way to transform you.

John O'Donohue (Irish poet and philosopher, 1956–2008)

94

ONLY GOOD

OVER A DECADE ago something momentous happened, changing my life forever – although I couldn't have known the change would be permanent. That the life I knew would be shattered. It was a beautiful sunny day when my first husband left our home with a suitcase, never to live under the same roof as me again. The circumstances were as complicated as the plot of the average opera, and since I told the story in my memoir (called *A Small Dog Saved My Life*) I don't need to revisit it.

The point I want to share is that when something like that happens, the carefully constructed house of cards tumbles down, and you survey the chaos crying helplessly, 'Why?' It can take years to begin to understand (first) that there are reasons for most of the unhappiness we endure, and (second) that the process of rebuilding those cards into a different structure can be so extraordinary that you can – in the end – almost feel grateful for the original disaster.

A few weeks ago, I had lunch with my first husband, and there wasn't enough time to catch up. We talked incessantly in the old, animated way, shared stories about our children, grandchildren and new lives, as well as our work – and it couldn't have been more lovely. Do I hear those of you who are still afflicted by bitterness after the end of a marriage (even years ago) mutter, 'Oh, it's all right for *her*' or 'Well, you're just *lucky*'?

Let me tell you, it *wasn't* all right and 'luck' is subject to imagination and hard work. I knew then what I know now, that I was lucky to have been married to that person for thirty-five years and that what we had shared was too precious to destroy through anger. The feeling is summed up in two lines from one of my favourite poets, the American, Edna St Vincent Millay:

> *Should I outlive this anguish – and men do –*
> *I shall have only good to say of you.*

Above all else, that is the message I try to convey – again and again – on this page. Which brings me to this month's second, equally special, anniversary. Seeing him also made me reflect on the accident that kicked me into a new career as an advice columnist and that change would never have happened had my first marriage not ended. The pain was necessary, you see, for the growth of a new vocation – which gives me more satisfaction than anything I have done in my life.

Yes – despite the sadness … 'only good'.

ACKNOWLEDGEMENTS

M Y BIGGEST DEBT is, of course, to the readers who go on challenging me but inspiring me too. I thank them for all they contribute to the newspaper and to my life.

I am very grateful to the editor of the *Daily Mail*, Paul Dacre, for giving permission for these extracts to be published, and want to thank him for his enthusiasm for the column and unfailing support. His genuine concern for what the readers want and believe is a lesson to any journalist.

I'm also grateful to other colleagues on the newspaper for their help and camaraderie. Although I work alone, far from the office, and rarely see them, I am glad that the *Mail* 'family' is there.

Without the quiet strength of my husband, Robin Allison-Smith, I would lack the fortitude to write, but he also bestows a lightness of heart that makes success and failure seem less important. He also knows exactly when a vodka and tonic is needed, to help me through. My family (parents, adult children, their lovely spouses and my grandchildren) continue to teach me how to love, be tolerant and have fun – and also that problems can be overcome with liberal applications of said fun, tolerance and love.

I would also like to thank my loyal friend Gaynor Rea for being the best cheerleader ever, in good times and bad. She knows what I mean. Finally, this book is dedicated to a colleague and friend who – in a light-bulb moment in 2005 when I met her for the first time – changed my life. A great believer in gratitude, I say thank you.